# RIDE! RIDE! RIDE!

## HERNE HILL VELODROME AND THE STORY OF BRITISH TRACK CYCLING

## MARK WELLINGS

Foreword by Graeme Obree

ICON

Published in the UK in 2016
by Icon Books Ltd, Omnibus Business Centre,
39–41 North Road, London N7 9DP
email: info@iconbooks.com
www.iconbooks.com

Sold in the UK, Europe and Asia
by Faber & Faber Ltd, Bloomsbury House,
74–77 Great Russell Street,
London WC1B 3DA or their agents

Distributed in the UK, Europe and Asia
by Grantham Book Services,
Trent Road, Grantham NG31 7XQ

Distributed in the USA
by Publishers Group West,
1700 Fourth Street, Berkeley, CA 94710

Distributed in Australia and New Zealand
by Allen & Unwin Pty Ltd,
PO Box 8500, 83 Alexander Street,
Crows Nest, NSW 2065

Distributed in South Africa
by Jonathan Ball, Office B4, The District,
41 Sir Lowry Road, Woodstock 7925

Distributed in India by Penguin Books India,
7th Floor, Infinity Tower – C, DLF Cyber City,
Gurgaon 122002, Haryana

Distributed in Canada by Publishers Group Canada,
76 Stafford Street, Unit 300
Toronto, Ontario M6J 2S1

ISBN: 978-178578-042-4

Typeset in Electra by Marie Doherty

Printed and bound in the UK
by Clays Ltd, St Ives plc

*The book is dedicated to my son Finlay for introducing me to the track, my daughter Monika for being my 'favourite daughter', and my wife Hilary for never-ending support during what turned out to be a much, much longer ride than I ever thought it would be.*

# Contents

# Contents

# Foreword

*by Graeme Obree*

I have fond personal memories of Herne Hill. I broke the British hour record there in 1993 and without that achievement my career in track cycling could easily have ended prematurely. It gave me the confidence to progress and beat Francesco Moser's hour world record on my own terms and have a cycling career that allowed me to compete all over the world.

Herne Hill Velodrome is such an important part of British cycling infrastructure and culture, allowing kids the opportunity to test out their skills on the track, giving them access to equipment and coaching that is often outwith their reach. The track at Hill Herne is also one for the connoisseurs. It is longer and shallower than modern-day velodromes, demanding different skill sets, tactics and intelligence.

But perhaps most significant of all, is the venue's heritage. It has been host to thousands of exciting races over the years and has witnessed incredible performances from the likes of Reg Harris, Fausto Coppi and Jacques Anquetil, Bradley Wiggins and Chris Boardman. It has enormous importance to the heritage of not only British cycling but also Continental track racing – it is to cycling what Lord's is to cricket.

Mark Wellings' affectionate portrayal of Herne Hill brings back great memories and helps keep this most important of British cycling venues alive.

Graeme Obree
March 2016

# Acknowledgements

I'm indebted to the help of many people who have known, loved and supported Herne Hill track over the years. First and foremost must be John and Christine Watts for their time and support, and for the exhaustive research John has done for his books on the velodrome and the Good Friday Meeting – both of which I have drawn on heavily.

Particular thanks also go to Jim Love for his stories and photographs, and also to Keith Robins, Wally Happy, Graham Bristow, Keith Waldegrave, Steve Cave, Pete Cattermole, Phil Wright and John Scripps for their time, thoughts and memories. I'm grateful also to Josh Cole-Hossain and Andrew Bradshaw for checking technical details in the book and more broadly for being inspirational young race promoters and coaches.

Thanks to editor and friend Ian Preece for persuading me to write the book in the first place and then providing enthusiastic encouragement and insightful support over the two years it's taken; plus Andrew Furlow, Duncan Heath, Robert Sharman and all the team at Icon Books.

Finally, cheers go to my favourite riding buddies Kev, Dom, Sean and everyone at VC Londres.

# Warm-up

Track cycling is one of the oldest and most special-
ised forms of cycle racing, featuring an eclectic mix of sprint
and endurance events for individuals and groups of riders.
Intense, physical and cerebral – track cycling is all about
speed, technique, tactics and nerve.

The bikes are strong and rigid to cope with extreme acceleration, with a single fixed gear (preventing freewheeling)
and no brakes. It is the simplest and purest bicycle, where
man is at one with machine.

The tracks themselves vary from large open-air oval circuits with shallow banking to the small, tight and steeply
banked hardwood ovals of the indoor velodromes.

And Herne Hill is arguably the best-known, most-loved
velodrome in the world with the richest history, ranking
alongside the legendary Velodromo Vignorelli in Milan,
Roubaix in northern France and Buffalo in Paris.

Known initially as Herne Hill Stadium when it was built
in 1891, and latterly Herne Hill Velodrome, but often referred

to simply as Herne Hill track or 'the Hill', it was for many years the leading international track in the UK. It is now the only remaining venue from the 1948 Olympics, with a direct link to 125 years of cycle racing: a unique and iconic institution, with a vibrant role and a bright future. It is simply the spiritual home of British track cycling.

*'Ride your bike, ride your bike, ride your bike'*
— Fausto Coppi on how to become a champion

# When two roads diverge

Two great cycle racing institutions were born in 1903: the Good Friday Meeting at Herne Hill in south London and the Tour de France across the Channel.

The Tour de France is not only the oldest and most prestigious of the three Grand Tour road stage races, it's grown to become the world's biggest annual sporting event. Traditionally held over three weeks in July and nowadays taking in a 3,500-kilometre circuit of France (and neighbouring countries), the first edition was 2,428 kilometres from Paris to Lyon, Marseille, Toulouse, Bordeaux, Nantes and back to Paris. It was won by Maurice Garin. The list of winners since then includes the greats of world cycling such as Fausto Coppi, Jacques Anquetil, Eddy Merckx, Bernard Hinault and Miguel Indurain, as well as Britain's Bradley Wiggins and Chris Froome.

The inaugural Good Friday Meeting, meanwhile, took place on an outdoor cycle track in suburban south London on 10 April 1903, some three months earlier. Herne Hill stadium stood in nine acres of grounds, modestly concealed from the general public by the recently built houses on Burbage Road to the south, Village Way in Dulwich to the east and a railway viaduct to the north – an inauspicious location for the most prestigious outdoor cycling track in the UK, one that was for many years the only international-standard track in the country, and one which is still revered by many as the spiritual home of track cycling in the United Kingdom.

Yet this venue has also been a showcase for the world's greatest cycle racing stars, witnessing the breaking of national and world records for 125 years: from Jimmy Michael, Leon Meredith and Frank Southall in the early days through Reg Harris, Tom Simpson and Barry Hoban and on to Tony Doyle, Graeme Obree, Bradley Wiggins and other leading lights of the 21st-century British cycling phenomenon. And that's just the British talent. There was also a panoply of foreign riders who appeared week in, week out, from Fausto Coppi to Jef Scherens, Toni Merkens and Stuart O'Grady.

For both events to continue through to this day with almost unbroken regularity is a remarkable achievement. But they also symbolise the divide that separated the UK and continental Europe for the following half-century. In Europe whole villages would turn out to watch hugely popular, colourful pelotons storming along public roads on free-wheel, multi-speed bikes. In the UK thousands would flock to noisy and colourful grass and hard tracks for virtuoso displays of

speed, risk-taking and endurance, on fixed-wheel bikes with
no brakes.

❀

The Good Friday Meeting was promoted by the Southern
Counties Cycling Union (SCCU) – an amateur association of
about 30 affiliated cycle clubs based in south London, Surrey
and Sussex, committed to organising track racing. Given that
there were already many race meetings and other distractions
over the Easter weekend and any form of public entertainment on Good Friday itself was generally discouraged, it was
a big risk for the modestly funded SCCU to launch a new
track meeting in 1903.

One of the first to sign up was Leon Meredith, the outstanding racing cyclist of the period. The London-born rider
was already the 50-mile national tandem-paced champion
at the time. A mild-looking, bespectacled man who parted
his thick black hair in the centre, his appearance belied a
tough character. In the following year, 1904, he won his first
world championship at Crystal Palace in the 100-kilometre
motor-paced event. As he entered the final 20 kilometres his
pacing motorcycle broke down and Meredith hit the banking
and fell. He turned somersaults across the track, but quickly
jumped back on to his feet covered in blood, shouted for
another bike and pacer and finished the race – breaking the
world amateur record to boot! He later went on to win two
Olympic medals and seven motor-paced world championships between 1904 and 1913 – still an unbeaten British record.

Other champions followed, to guarantee a high-class field.
Vic Johnson, a thick-set carpenter from Warwickshire with a
low hairline and protruding ears, was a brilliant sprinter who
went on win a sprint gold medal at the 1908 Olympics and
also became world amateur sprint champion, and holder of
three world records. The diminutive A.E. Wills, also known
as the 'Putney flyer', was another brilliant amateur racer,
who went on to find fame as the first ever rider to break the
mile-a-minute barrier for an hour, managing 60mph paced
cycling from a standing start at a Munich track in 1908.

But despite a high-class field, crowds were by no means
guaranteed as track racing was actually in a period of relative
decline following the 1890s heyday. Cycling had been hugely
popular as pastime and sport in the closing decade of the
19th century, after the invention of the safety bicycle (the
precursor of the modern bike), but crowds were starting to
drift away as the craze ran its course with the fickle general
public. In his research for *The Good Friday Gamble*, John
Watts unearthed the memoirs of Aubrey King, a member of
the De Laune Cycle Club, who recalled meeting at the Half
Moon pub near Herne Hill station beforehand with a group
of anxious officials and helpers. The meeting had been well
promoted, with a good programme and fine weather too, but
they still feared failure.

" Imagine our astonishment when we sauntered into
Burbage Road to find a queue five to six deep stretching beyond the railway arches with more and more

people hurrying to join. Our saunter broke into a run and it was a stiff job forcing our way into the ground. Half a dozen stewards opened the big gates and the money was thrown into sacks as the spectators poured through. By two o'clock every seat was taken, the enclosures packed and a deep circle all round the ground. 🎵

It would have been a mixed crowd: predominantly men dressed in black top hats with long dark coats to protect them against the spring chill in the grandstand; but also the middle classes in their bowler hats, and the working classes in their flat caps milling around the cheaper viewing areas. And lurking among them was a risk which became apparent when the racing started. No horse racing was allowed on Good Friday; consequently, 'half the bookmakers in south London had come along to combine business with pleasure' and when the first heat started 'the shouting of odds drowned everything else'.

The race promoters would be held responsible for breaking the law, meaning the meeting itself would be under threat – not to mention their investment. King described the robust response from the organisers:

> 🎵 We pleaded and threatened but it was no use; so with our one sergeant, two constables and every available steward we bundled the ringleaders outside the enclosure and locked the gates. But as soon as our backs

were turned they tore up one of the long seats and forced the gate off its hinges to get back again. Things certainly looked ugly when we went after them, and it was a hard struggle before they were deposited outside the ground. Most of us bore the mark of battle and my chum, a big Scandinavian cyclist, had his right eye closed, but he enjoyed every minute of the fun. Anyway, it stopped the betting and the crowd settled down to an exciting afternoon of sport. 🙶

The racing itself was enthusiastically cheered on by the capacity crowd, according to Watts' reviews of the press reports, especially the shorter races. The quarter-mile and half-mile handicaps were both hotly contested. G.C. Anderson of West Ham was narrowly beaten by W. East of Paddington CC in the quarter-mile, but then went on to win the half-mile by half a wheel.

There were eleven riders competing for the Mellins Cup in the 10 miles point-to-point race (an endurance race which encourages speed and excitement by awarding points for intermediate sprint laps, with the winner being the rider who accumulates the most points, not necessarily the first over the line at the end), including numerous national champions. Meredith was beaten into second by Wills, who also went on to win the race in the two following years, giving him the right to take the trophy home for keeps.

'Never in the whole annals of track cycling, has a meeting been so largely attended nor the field so good in each event,' sang the praise in *Cycling* magazine, 'to say nothing of the keenness of the competition, as at a Good Friday gathering.' Happily it was no flash in the pan. The following year saw record crowds again ('the road to the track was like the Epsom road on Derby day,' according to press reports) and the meeting went from strength to strength.

# 2

# Fast and loose

# 2

## Fast and furious

British cycling success may feel like a recent phenomenon, with 21st-century Olympic gold medallists, world champions and Tour de France winners – and British cycling is certainly enjoying a golden era – but it has a glorious record, right back to the dawn of bike racing in the 1860s.

The world's first officially organised cycle race is immortalised as the one held in Parc de Saint-Cloud on the banks of the Seine in western Paris on 31 May 1868. And it was won by James Moore, an Englishman – albeit one who had lived in Paris since he was five years old, when his father moved there from Bury St Edmunds in Suffolk to work as a blacksmith and farrier.

The bicycle had evolved from its early days in 1818 when a Paris-based German, Baron Karl Friedrich Drais von Sauerbronn, had patented his running machine – the so-called 'Draisienne'. This was basically a wooden two-wheeler with a saddle and handlebars, propelled along by the riders' legs – a simple, winning format still sold as 'balance bicycles' for young children today. Denis Johnson of London swiftly evolved the design to include an elegant curved wooden frame and metal parts which made it lighter than its predecessor. He also showed far more entrepreneurial flair when his 'pedestrian curricle' as it was called, became very popular with Regency dandies, earning the more memorable nicknames 'hobby-horse' or 'dandy-horse'.

The next major development was in 1861, in Paris again, when Pierre Michaux a French blacksmith, attached pedals and cranks to the front wheel of a dandy-horse and called his invention a 'velocipede'. This innovation enabled mechanically transmitted leg power: a game-changer in the evolution of the bicycle. Although they were branded velocipedes, once ridden on cobbled streets or stony tracks they quickly became known as 'boneshakers' for obvious reasons.

The velocipedes used in the Parc de Saint-Cloud race in 1868 were huge and heavy wooden machines with wheels of flattened metal: a 31-inch back wheel and a 38-inch front wheel. Napoleon III bought one and gave a dozen to his aristocratic friends, who took to them straight away. They quickly became popular with young, wealthy Parisians and began to be mass-produced by firms such as Michaux's.

The event in Parc de Saint-Cloud was organised by René and Aimé Olivier, owners of the Compagnie Parisienne, who had recently acquired the Michaux company from the family, and wanted publicity for their new product. By this stage the factory was turning out over 400 machines a year. The event was well advertised, with generous prizes, was open to all-comers and brought a large, enthusiastic and well-heeled crowd, dressed in crinolines, top hats and frock coats.

Somewhere between five and ten riders are reported to have lined up between two ornamental fountains on the gravel path in the park, according to research by cycling historian Les Woodland. They raced 600 metres, turned and raced back. Francois Drouet, the favourite, took an early lead, followed by a rider named Palocini, but at the halfway turning point Moore 'accelerated as fast as lightning' according to the *Cycling Record*, winning by 20 metres. He was cheered with 'frenetic hurrahs' and won a gold medal worth 100 francs, engraved with his name and the image of Napoleon III.

While the occasion has gone down in folklore as the first ever bike race, there's actually debate over whether it was even the first race on the day – and there is some evidence that organised races may have been held before this date too – but nonetheless, it's this race and this rider that have stolen the limelight. In its write-up of the afternoon's racing, *Le Petit-Journal* also reported a 50-metre 'slow race' for six competitors.

> This race was very amusing; the riders tried their best not to go fast, without stopping; their contrary movements made them fall except for Mr J Darenty, student of the Grand Gymnasium, who won the prize.

Cyclists were already developing a passion for arcane and eclectic race formats.

Cycle racing had caught the public imagination else-where too and soon inspired similar events in the UK and Belgium. The first formal cycle race in England was held on 1 June 1868 – the very next day – in less salubrious surroundings: a field behind the Welsh Harp Hotel, a public house in Hendon, north London. It was won by Arthur Markham, who received a silver cup from the licensee of the hotel, who had sponsored the race. Markham went on to open bicycle shops in Edgware Road and Shepherd's Bush, and had the occasional brush with the law for running fraudulent bike races.

But the bicycle had been adopted much earlier in France and racing quickly grew in popularity there. Despite the excitement of the crowds at Saint-Cloud, the races were actually quite slow: very low gearing essentially limited the speed to how fast riders could spin their legs. The challenge therefore turned from how fast a rider could go, to how far. The Olivier brothers, fresh from the success of their first race came up with the idea of a long-distance race from Paris to Rouen. Mass-start cycle racing was born. And James Moore won this one too. Held on 7 November 1869, the one-day race ran from the Arc de Triomphe in Paris to Rouen (81 miles), and took in St-Germain, Mantes, Vernon and Louviers. One of the few rules stated that riders were 'not to be trailed by a dog or use sails'. The event was sponsored by sports newspaper *Le Velocipede Illustre*, a tradition that continued on to 1903 when *L'Auto* sports paper sponsored the first Tour de France.

Cycles evolved quickly in the eighteen months following Parc de Saint-Cloud and by the time of the Paris–Rouen race, metal frames and metal-spoked wheels were common; tyres were made of rubber and the hubs ran on ball bearings. Speed was still limited by the rider's leg speed as he turned the front wheel, so the bigger the wheel, the greater the distance travelled per pedal revolution. Wheels grew to enormous sizes – resulting in the development of the 'ordinary' or 'penny-farthing'. With saddles over five feet from the floor, penny-farthings were the preserve of daring young racers – generally male. Moore's bike had a 48-inch front wheel and 15-inch rear wheel.

The first prize was 1,000 francs, and 120 starters, including several women, set off from Paris at 7am. This is the first record of women's cycle racing, although there is discrepancy over how many there were. Moore was the favourite, alongside Jean-Eugène-André Castéra, who had come second at Saint-Cloud, and another Englishman, a visiting student from Cambridge called Johnson. Moore won in 10 hours, 25 minutes (an average speed of 8mph), 15 minutes ahead of his nearest competitor. Only 34 competitors made it inside the time limit, including one woman, in 22nd place. Although female competitors were welcomed by organisers in this and other early races, in wider society cycling was still regarded as a scandalous activity for women, so the finisher called herself 'Miss America', rather than using her real name (and despite apparently being English!).

Possibly one of the reasons the Saint-Cloud race has dominated historical memory is the fact that Moore went on to become one of the first stars of cycle racing, dominating competition for many years. As well as winning Paris–Rouen, he became the first ever world champion when he won the MacGregor Cup in 1872, retaining it in 1873, 1874, 1875 and 1877. He also won the one-mile world championships in 1874 at the purpose-built track at Molineux Pleasure Grounds in Wolverhampton, where he also set an 'hour record' of 14 miles, 880 yards.

After the invention of the ordinary, which enabled much longer trips to be made, the bicycle soon became popular for leisure as well as competition. The introduction of solid rubber tyres improved comfort and handling even further. Although Britain was behind France in its adoption of the bike, cycling quickly gained in popularity. In February 1869 three cyclists – Rowley Turner, John Mayall and Charles Spencer – rode from London to Brighton, trailed by a reporter from *The Times*. It took them 15 hours to cover the 53 miles: a mere 3.5mph, but that did little to dampen *The Times*' enthusiasm when it proclaimed the 'Extraordinary velocipede feat'.

Meanwhile, Jerome K. Jerome, author of *Three Men in a Boat*, wrote that

> ❝ In Battersea Park, any morning between eleven and one, all the best blood in England could be seen, solemnly pedalling up and down the half-mile drive that runs between the river and the refreshment kiosk. But these were the experts – the finished article. In

shady by-paths, elderly countesses, perspiring peers, still in the wobbly stage, battled bravely with the laws of equilibrium. "

But in reality cyclists were quickly becoming quite unpopular with large sections of the general public as they thundered through villages blowing their bugles, horns and whistles to warn people and sleeping dogs of their approach. To put things in context, motor cars weren't allowed on public roads until 1896 or to exceed 12mph until 1903: a limit which also applied to cycles.

Many people resented swarms of cyclists riding furiously along the roads endangering life and tranquillity. The riders crowded into quiet village post offices to send telegrams to prove how far they had ridden and frequently behaved in an arrogant and discourteous manner. Rivalry soon developed, with village lads ambushing cyclists, encouraging aggravated dogs to attack cyclists, poking sticks through their wheels or even stretching wire across quiet lanes to bring them down. In 1876 Henry Cracknel, the driver of the St Albans mail coach was fined for swinging a home-made weapon made from ropes and weights out of his window, bringing down the entire Trafalgar Bicycle Club.

More and more cyclists were also taking part in competitive events. Road races rapidly evolved from informal affairs into organised challenges. One of the first promoters was the North Road Club, formed in 1885 'to promote fast and long-distance cycling on the Great North and other roads'.

Road races also started the practice of using pacers, instantly doubling the number of riders charging for the line.

The fact that cycling, as both pastime and sport, was mainly the preserve of the aristocracy didn't seem to make any difference to the authorities' disapproving attitude. In 1878 a proposed change to the Highways Act would have made cycling illegal. Although the law was not changed, the police took to more actively harassing 'road scorchers'. They often adopted a hard-line approach, charging at racers on horseback and throwing truncheons into wheels. In 1882, *The Cyclist* magazine reported on a gentleman of a 'most respectable address' being fined 40 shillings for riding through London at a 'furious' 10mph.

The restrictions led to a drive to find alternative places to race: better surfaces, in private and without interference from the police. Races were held on closed circuits, tracks or 'paths' – made of ash, shale, gravel, grass and eventually cement – partly as a result of health and safety concerns, partly as a way to commercialise racing as a spectator sport. Many of the earliest events were held in general sports arenas, but soon special tracks or 'velodromes' were constructed. In the second half of the 19th century, velodromes had begun to appear across Europe and the United States. Soon, they sprang up all over the United Kingdom, with more than twenty in London alone.

As sports grounds became enclosed in the 1870s and

people began to have to pay for the pleasure of watching horse racing, rabbit-coursing or dog racing, attendance initially went down. But cycle racing was a popular spectator sport from its earliest days: the novelty and sensationalism meant it was one of the few events to attract large crowds and fascinate the press. The races were carefully orchestrated and hugely popular, with 15,000+ crowds turning up at velodromes and adapted exhibition halls to watch the action and bet on the results with trackside bookies.

Track cycle racing was in full swing, with events at enclosed grounds such as the Star Grounds in Fulham or Aston Cross Grounds in Birmingham. Penny-farthing races were mostly held on big flat cinder tracks, one of the most famous being Lillie Bridge track in Chelsea. In 1875, 'monster crowds' of 18,000 were reported at Wolverhampton's Molineux Pleasure Grounds during the Christmas period to watch cycling stars compete.

Wolverhampton had quickly become a centre for bicycle manufacturing and Oliver McGregor, an astute local businessman and owner of Molineux House and grounds, realised the potential of organised cycle races – both as a way of raising money through entrance fees, but also stimulating interest in buying the new machines. In the late 1860s he built a cycle track around an ornamental boating lake and fountain, and began promoting regular race meetings several times a week, with large prizes. The track was one of the best in the country for a number of years, hosting many international race meetings including the international bicycle world championships in 1886, before being built over to become the home ground for Wolverhampton Wanderers FC in 1889 – the new craze.

In 1878 the Cyclists' Touring Club was founded, with membership going on to reach its peak of 60,000 in 1899. The Pickwick Bicycle Club, together with Cambridge University Bicycle Club and two others, also formed the Bicycle Union in the Guildhall Tavern, London in 1878. It was set up to oversee bicycle racing in all its forms. They hosted the first official British National Cycling Championships in May 1878 at the Stamford Bridge arena, later to become home to Chelsea FC. The two-mile event was won by Ion Keith-Falconer, a six-foot three-inch Edinburgh-born, Harrow-educated Cambridge University student, allowing him to lay claim to being Britain's first cycling champion, if not the fastest cyclist in the world.

Keith-Falconer had been winning cycle races since he'd started competing in 1874. He enjoyed a decade or so of success on road and track, including riding from Land's End to John o'Groats in thirteen days, finishing his cycling career at the amateur championship in 1882 at Crystal Palace. He went on to become a professor of Arabic at Cambridge University and later a missionary, which gives a clue as to his naively optimistic attitude towards the benefits of cycling, picked up by Carlton Reid in his fascinating book *Roads Were Not Built for Cars*:

    ❝  It is an excellent thing to encourage an innocent sport (such as bicycling) which keeps young fellows out of the public-houses, music halls and gambling hells and all the other traps that are ready to catch them. It is a great advantage to enter for a few races in public, and not merely to ride on the road for exercise, because in the former case one has to train oneself and this involves abstinence from beer and wine and tobacco, and early going to bed and early rising, and gets one's body into a really vigorous, healthy state. As to betting, nearly all Clubs forbid it, strictly … A bicycle race-course is as quiet as a public science lecture. 〞

❋

An iconic track racing format that would no doubt have horrified and appalled Keith-Falconer at the time but was to gain huge popularity also started in the 1870s. Six-day racing began as a stunt, playing to popular taste in late Victorian England for unusual, callous tests of physical strength and stamina. This was an era when prizefighting was illegal but still practised. In 1860 a bare-knuckle fight between an Englishman, Tom Sayers, and an American, John C. Heenan, was staged in Farnborough, Hampshire and reportedly continued into the 42nd round before the mob broke it up. It was the qualities of strength and endurance that appealed to spectators, rather than skill per se.

Six-day racing took the specific form it did due to public respect for the Sabbath. Keeping Sunday a day of rest was supported by law and observed so strictly that there was debate over whether it was acceptable to ride a bicycle in public at all on Sundays, even for recreation or transport – never mind racing. So if the endurance of cyclists was to be tested to its limit, the longest period it could be done for was between midnight on a Sunday and midnight the following Saturday. (The principles still apply today, although it's rare for six-day races *not* to run through Sundays nowadays, as that's a busy day for crowds.)

There's a lot of speculation about when and where the first six-day races were held – and indeed what format they took – but the events have a history going back at least as far as Birmingham in 1875, when riders set out to cycle around an oval timber outdoor track for twelve hours a day. That event was organised by a local manufacturer of ordinaries who wanted to demonstrate the reliability of his products. Another, eighteen-hour event, held in London later in the year was won by eighteen-year-old George Waller. The runner-up was Charles Terront, an eighteen-year-old Frenchman, who went on to become the first French cycling star, winning 54 major sprint, middle-distance and endurance events in Europe and the United States over a fifteen-year career.

These early races were essentially promotional events, but three years later the first recognised six-day races were held at the Royal Agricultural Hall (now the Business Design Centre) in Islington, London in 1878. Indoor races had been held there – albeit with the venue renamed the Velocipede Cirque for the occasion – as early as 1869.

The late Victorians' love of excess and watching suffering

led to a variety of formats being tried – a six-day walking contest in April 1877 reportedly attracted crowds of 20,000 a day. A more direct precursor of the race format was held in February 1878 when a professional rider called David Stanton sought a bet that he could ride 1,000 miles in less than six days, riding no more than eighteen hours a day. It was essentially an individual time trial over six days, with a £100 stake put up by a Mr Davis and held by the *Sporting Life* newspaper. A flat oval track was marked around the Royal Agricultural Hall interior and he started riding his penny-farthing at 6am on 25 February. He hit 1,000 miles and won the bet in 73 hours, riding at an average speed of 13.5mph.

It may not sound much of a spectacle, but Londoners flocked to it. Another six-day race took place at the same venue in September 1878, this time with competitors: pitting a horse rider against cyclists for eleven hours a day. It was won by a Mexican called Leon riding the horse, who managed 969 miles – 59 miles more than his nearest bike-riding competitor, Bill Cann, 'Champion of the north', from Sheffield. Although there was much argument as Leon had been allowed to change horses.

That event inspired a six-day race for cyclists in November 1878. The potential for calamitous falls at high speed was assumed to be a clear crowd-pleaser. The prizes were substantial: £100 for the winner, £25 for second, £15 for third and £10 for fourth. The twelve riders, wearing tight trousers with stockings to the knees, rode penny-farthings around a tiny temporary track, also at the Royal Agricultural Hall, without banking or even fencing to separate them from the raucous spectators. It was not a man-to-man battle so much as an endurance challenge (the racing was limited to eighteen hours a day, 6am–midnight) to be undertaken at whatever time and speed the competitors felt they could achieve their best performance. According to race reports cited by Woodland only four started at 6am on the first day and despite 'rattling away in fine style', heavy falls soon came thick and fast.

The eventual winner was Cann, who managed 1,060 miles. Like the other British racers he was contemptuous of the French rider Terront, who worked as a bike messenger when he wasn't racing and was therefore considered scandalously professional. After failing to get rid of the Frenchman by ganging up on him, the British riders called a truce and offered flowers as a conciliation (it being assumed that Frenchmen liked that sort of thing), but when they enthusiastically coaxed him into smelling the gift Terront accused them of peppering the flowers with sleeping powder! Ultimately, though, he lost the race in part due to poor planning – he left the stadium to eat at cafés when he was hungry, whereas the British riders had food brought to them.

By 1879 there were six-day races in Birmingham and Hull, and by the following year they had spread to cities across the UK. The races became a hugely popular spectator sport in the closing years of the 19th century, with the format spreading beyond Britain to Europe and the United States.

They were usually held on temporary indoor tracks, rather

than the outdoor velodromes. Some tracks were so tiny and their banks so steep that they looked like walls of death. The riders would race individually for fourteen to eighteen hours a day over six days. The race went on non-stop and riders would snatch a bit of sleep here and there when they could, but 'the clock was always ticking'.

At first the spectacle just revolved around watching the suffering as the week went on, but the taste grew for faster and faster racing and crashes were inevitable and popular. There was constant noise from the drunken, smoking crowds, hired bands, public address megaphones, all crammed into the centre as well as the outer. There was a freak show and fairground atmosphere to cycle racing. Racers were coerced into getting back on to their bikes after the inevitable crashes and collapses. Those who finished were exhausted, dazed or hallucinating.

All-women races were introduced to add novelty and glamour, with the women also riding two to eight hours a day, wearing divided skirts or knickerbockers and voluminous blouses. Women had been involved in track racing in France as early as the 1860s and usually had their own races at the end of the programme. The combination of athleticism and femininity seems to have given a major boost to profits. The riders were generally actresses and acrobats, but also wayward daughters of the bourgeoisie. The initial forays into women's races were patchy, but by the late 1890s it was more common, coinciding with the development of the safety cycle.

In 1896 a troupe of visiting French female cyclists,

performing exhibitions of speed and skill at the Royal Aquarium in London, earned more than their male counterparts – mainly as they were pounced upon by agents and cycle manufacturers keen to encourage their participation. The combination of expenses, appearance fees and prize money sometimes totalled well over £100 a week.

But the races weren't simply for the male spectators' titillation, according to cycling historian and sociologist Dave Horton. He quotes Josiah Ritchie, managing director of the Royal Aquarium, describing the women's races, which 'aroused the keenest interest amongst ladies even of the aristocracy, and there were often to be seen edging our track quite as many "picture hats" as prosaic "bowlers" and "toppers".'

Cycles themselves were going from strength to strength as the design and engineering was finessed. By the mid-1870s, Britain joined the chase to design and produce a machine that was safer than the penny-farthing.

In 1874 Henry John Lawson produced a bicycle with two wheels of roughly equal and moderate size and a double-diamond frame; a chain-ring with pedals and cranks drove a smaller sprocket attached to the rear wheel, making several revolutions per single revolution of the crank. There was no longer any need for the penny-farthing's huge front wheel: the 'safety bicycle' was born – basically the blueprint for bikes today; bikes that could be safely and decorously ridden by both sexes.

The bicycle was one of the most exciting and influential technological developments of the 19th century. It soon came to symbolise freedom, and in particular it made women independently mobile for the first time. But as James McGurn's research of contemporary media revealed, not everyone approved of ladies riding, never mind racing. 'Few will contend that the lady cyclist is a thing of beauty,' ranted *Woman* magazine. 'The pedal action is too like the rhythmic swing of a carpet beater, and … the shapeless garments in no way [suggest] personal cleanliness.'

In Belfast in 1887, John Boyd Dunlop invented the pneumatic bicycle tyre which replaced the solid rubber tyres, making riding on the open road a lot more attractive. First used in racing in 1889, the air-filled tyres were an instant success. So by the late 1880s the development of the low, rear-wheel-driven safety bicycle, with inflatable tyres, had effectively ended the reign of the high-wheel bikes – although traditionalists and purists persisted with riding ordinaries.

Cycling became the height of fashion, led by aristocrats, celebrities and the conspicuously wealthy. In 1870 the Pickwick Bicycle Club had been founded in Hackney Downs (in honour of the recently deceased Dickens), swiftly followed by clubs in Edinburgh, Surrey, Oxford and Cambridge. Club membership was small and exclusive as the machines were not cheap at that time, so cycling was still restricted to members of the middle and upper classes. Bicycles cost from £10 for the lowest quality to £30 or more for the most deluxe; a good model was typically £20. A penny-farthing would have cost a working man the equivalent of ten weeks' wages.

But prices began to fall. The so-called Coventry Gentleman's Bicycle produced by James Starley of the Coventry Machinist Company (swiftly renamed from Coventry Sewing Machine Company to cater for the trend) cost £16 in 1875. By 1884, J. Durley of Wolverhampton was producing the Working Man's Friend at only £4 10s. In 1885 Starley responded with the Rover, which was even cheaper. By 1896 there would be as many as 700 British factories turning out variations on the same idea. France was still suffering the after-effects of the Franco-Prussian war and Coventry became the world capital of cycle making.

By the late-1890s the price of bikes came within reach of the better-off working classes, leading to a rise in club membership. Cycle clubs were booming all over the country, not just cycling for sport, but also as pastime with people going on tours, club runs and generally exploring the local areas as a social activity. Whereas in 1874 there were around 29 British clubs, by 1878 there were 189; by 1882 the number had risen to 528 and by the 1890s there were over 300 cycling clubs in London alone.

At this stage things were also coming to a head on the roads. The National Cyclists' Union (NCU) which grew out of the Bicycle Union and controlled all cycle racing at the time, sided with authority. In an attempt to curtail the rising opposition to cycling in general and fearing all cycling might be banned from the open road, the NCU voluntarily banned mass-start racing on public highways in 1890. The NCU prohibited their officials from assisting in any road races and refused to recognise any records or results on the road.

The National Cyclists' Union was a well-meaning organisation that saw cycling as a sport for gentleman, which is why it fell into line with the police on mass-start races and insistence that racing cyclists should not receive a prize in cash, nor any prize that could be of use in cycling. Racing should be kept pure and amateur: for the love of competition and without any financial imperative.

It was a generally misguided move by the NCU, intended to more actively promote track racing, but which had repercussions for cycle racing that would rumble on for 50 years. However, the decision did have the desired effect of increasing the amount of track racing even further during the late 1880s and early 1890s. Although road racing was banned, it still took place and the authorities continued to clamp down. There were also far greater commercial opportunities in track racing. Cycle racing began to attract huge crowds. It was at this point that the idea for Herne Hill track was born.

# 3

## One continuous roar

Herne Hill stadium, or London County Grounds as it was officially known, opened in suburban south London on 23 May 1891. This was a period of great change: in 1891 the Dalton Gang and Wild Bunch were still robbing banks and trains in the Old West, while their countryman Thomas Edison patented the motion picture camera and Britain was first linked to the Continent by telephone. This was the same year that Crufts Dog Show began (also at the Royal Agricultural Hall in Islington), Sherlock Holmes first appeared in *The Strand Magazine* and *Cycling* magazine was founded – a magazine that still exists as *Cycling Weekly*, covering racing at Herne Hill to this day.

Back in the 1880s there were already over a dozen tracks or paths in the London area alone. Paths like the makeshift one used in 1868, behind the Welsh Harp Hotel in Hendon, had mushroomed into a plethora of temporary and permanent circuits on surfaces ranging from grass and cinders through to wood and cement. As racing became more and more popular, so the number of London tracks grew rapidly through the 1880s. Fulham, Chiswick, Crystal Palace, Surbiton, Alexandra Palace, Kennington, Wood Green, Paddington, Kensal Rise, Balham, Bow Grounds, Stamford Bridge and Sheen all held regular race meetings.

But velodromes built in Britain during this period rarely met with commercial success; the intense enthusiasm only lasted a few years and by the turn of the century many had closed down. Yet Herne Hill was to survive and thrive, becoming the leading centre of track cycling in the UK for many years.

It was George Lacy Hillier who had the idea and ambition to build a great new south London venue. He was an amateur racing cyclist, race organiser, journalist and stockbroker, who felt that the nearby Crystal Palace track, built in 1880, had reached the end of its useful life. Subsidence was taking place and it was not banked, so it wasn't suitable for the increasingly high speeds of the new safety bikes.

There was a clear commercial argument too: the opportunity to physically enclose the racing meant that organisers and promoters could charge for entry, in a way that hadn't been possible when races took place in public parks, roads or countryside. Sixpence, for example, provided open access to the whole of Crystal Palace park and all activities at the time, which included gardens, lakes and fountains, a maze, an aquarium and countless statues including 33 life-sized models of the newly discovered dinosaurs in the park. Track racing also gave spectators the chance to focus on the spectacle for longer, whereas in a road race the riders passed just once.

John Watts has researched and written about the early history of Herne Hill stadium in great depth. He quotes Hillier writing in *Bicycling News* of his ambitious plans to establish 'a really first-class track' – one to put all others in the shadows due to its speed, scale and excellent facilities: 'It would not do for the new path to be anyway behind its competitors; it will, we think, surpass them all in the comfort and completeness of its surroundings, as well as its size.' He got the support and financial backing of friends and colleagues, including William and John Peacock, owners of a building firm in Brixton and members of the Brixton Ramblers Cycling Club. The Peacock brothers were doing good business in the area during the housing boom, and had the money to invest in their pastime. They became the sole proprietors of the track for the next 50 years.

Hillier negotiated the right to build on nine acres of land occupied by a dairy farm, leased from the Dulwich Estate (a wealthy charitable foundation with origins dating back to 1619, when it was established by Edward Alleyn, a Shakespearian actor, for the purposes of educating and housing poor scholars). He brought on board Harry Swindley, a former racer and an authority on velodrome design and construction. The focus of attention was a 504-yard cycle track, with two 90-yard straights and shallow banking on semi-circular ends to allow speeds in excess of 25mph. It was made of finely crushed red stone, which when compressed after rolling, produced a hard, fast surface.

An impressive grandstand with cast-iron pillars and decorative fencing seated 220 spectators, while the two-storey brick building at its rear housed changing rooms, meeting rooms, offices and a bar. It was flanked by two more modest side stands, open to the elements and each seating a further 200-odd fans. A terraced standing area as the south banking entered the home straight provided further additional viewing for spectators. The track was surrounded by a three-foot-high white picket fence, interspersed with flagpoles. It was estimated that a continuous line of spectators around the perimeter fence, one person deep, roughly equated to a further 1,000 spectators.

As with many stadiums of the time, the cycle track surrounded a 440-yard cinder running track with four lanes. A judges' box was on the inside of the track at the finish line, while there was also a press area, refreshments and a bike park on the outside by the home straight, and a second refreshment tent on the back straight. There were also gas lights for night-time training – or 24-hour record attempts.

A double row of trees in a semi-circle following the curve of the track on the grandstand side came to be euphemistically described as a 'Lovers' walk'. But as a state-of-the-art Victorian facility, it more than justified Hillier's ambition.

The first racing at Herne Hill took place on Thursday 16 April 1891, contested by members of the newly formed London County Cycling and Athletic Club. The inaugural race that evening, a two-mile handicap for ordinaries, was won by Ernest Osmond, the National Cyclists' Union champion from 1887 to 1891, who later went on to break the world two-mile safety record, also at Herne Hill, in August 1893. For the time being, though, Hillier showed a clear bias against the safety bike: at the public opening on Saturday 23 May, all but one race was for his beloved ordinaries.

Hillier's reputation, connections and organisational ability ensured leading riders would compete in a series of successful races. Records were quickly broken on the track, and in November 1891 Montague Holbein, a native of south London who had finished runner-up in the first Bordeaux–Paris cycle race earlier that year, and one of the leading long-distance riders of the day, attempted the 24-hour record.

Holbein was a large, muscular man, with a fashionable handlebar moustache. He had a team of pacers mounted on safeties, ordinaries, tandems and tandem tricycles to help him, and rode through the night illuminated by the gas lamps around the circuit, while a Wells light (a large, portable paraffin lamp) roared away in the centre. He successfully broke the record, covering 326 miles in 24 hours. (Holbein changed allegiance to endurance swimming after a few years and was described by *The Spectator* in 1903 as 'once a champion cyclist, now probably the strongest swimmer in the world', when he made one of numerous attempts to swim the English Channel.)

Building on the success of the new record, Hillier organised a paced 24-hour challenge cup, sponsored by chocolate and cocoa manufacturers Root & Co. The first Cuca Cocoa Challenge Cup, held in July 1892, was won by Frank Shorland from Northamptonshire riding a geared ordinary, with a distance of almost 414 miles – smashing Holbein's record. Shorland was a nephew of Jerome K. Jerome and a London–Brighton record holder in 1890. Like many pioneer racing cyclists he went on to enjoy a successful career in the motor industry, Charles Rolls being the more famous example. Shorland won the Cuca Cup again in 1893 and also 1894, when he covered 426 miles 400 yards on a safety. An improvement of 100 miles in only three years underlined the phenomenal pace of improvement in bicycle technology at this time.

In the constant search for speed, most middle- and long-distance track races were paced by teams on tandems – triplets, quadruplets and even quintuplets – with the racers (known as 'stayers') following as close as possible to profit from the slipstream of the pacer. Riders would have teams of pacers to swap over during the race, to ensure maximum speeds were maintained over long durations. People flocked to the tracks to watch these races. As time wore on, even the pacers were often top-class racers near the end of their careers who realised they could earn more in pacing teams than in continuing to race.

Hillier proudly declared Herne Hill to be 'the fastest track in the world' – although within a short space of time the consensus was that cement was actually the faster surface. The first cement track in the country had opened in Putney in August 1891, only three months after Herne Hill, and other cement tracks soon were opening in Europe, including the Vélodrome Buffalo in Paris (the name coming from the Wild West showman Buffalo Bill Cody, whose circus played on the grounds of the track).

By spring 1893 they decided to change the track surface at Herne Hill too, but rather than cement, the owners opted for pitch pine planks with the joints filled with cork. That was a seemingly odd choice for an outdoor track in the UK, but at the time planks were considered easy to lay, without foundation, and could be lifted and stored in winter. The wood yielded a fast surface and later in the year Jack Stocks, sporting the mandatory handlebar moustache, rode 25 miles and 360 yards in an hour – the first rider to break 25 miles within one hour. Stocks went on to become a professional rider in the late 1890s. In 1897, riding with pacers on the Crystal Palace track (which by this time had added banking), he broke all the cycle records from six to 32 miles inclusive. He also broke the hour record again, cycling 32¾ miles.

But records weren't only being broken at Herne Hill. In May 1893 at a race meeting at the Harlequins Sports Ground in Cardiff, a young amateur Welsh rider called Arthur Linton made history by breaking all Welsh records from five to 22 miles, and the unpaced world hour record. As a result, he was invited to make his London debut, competing at Herne Hill in the second 24-hour Cuca Cocoa Challenge Cup in July of that year. There were eighteen competitors, fourteen on safeties and four on tricycles. The favourite was once again Frank Shorland, the previous year's winner, who was by now established as one of England's best long-distance riders.

Arthur Linton had been born in Somerset in 1868, but his family moved to South Wales when he was only three. He grew up in the Welsh coal mining village of Aberaman, and began working down the mine himself at the age of twelve. But while still a teenager he started to make a name for himself as a cyclist.

Linton was strong from the gun and pushed Shorland hard over the first 100 miles, but then began to fade through lack of food and disorganised pacing. He ultimately failed to finish, but impressed everyone with his strength, courage and determination. His talent was widely recognised and a few weeks later he appeared at Herne Hill again in the twelve-hour Anchor Shield. Once more showing his inexperience, he led from the gun against seasoned riders like A.W. Horton and C.G. Ridgeway, covering the first 200 miles in just over ten hours. But once again he faded, and eventually finished third.

In October, on his third attempt at Herne Hill, Linton made a successful attempt on the British 100-mile record. Despite many punctures and even more disorganised pacing, he set a new record of 4 hours and 29 minutes. He had made a huge impact through raw talent, courage and determination, but knew that he needed expert coaching to go any further. He turned professional and started working with James Edward 'Choppy' Warburton, a cycling coach who was beginning to acquire the reputation for being the best, and certainly the most high-profile, in the business.

Warburton immediately recognised Linton's innate talent, so he put him under contract with the Gladiator team in Paris and started building the rider's reputation, albeit in a very late Victorian manner. Nicknaming him 'The Collier Boy', he set up a showcase race against 'Buffalo Bill' Cody, whose Wild West Show was in Paris at the time and involved Buffalo Bill riding a horse. Cody's top star Annie Oakley, meanwhile, would show off her shooting prowess from the saddle of a bicycle.

Linton's brothers Tom and Sam also joined the Warburton group, and in 1894 they were followed by yet another teammate from the Aberaman Cycling Club, Jimmy Michael, who had also burst on to the scene to make his mark at Herne Hill.

From the Rhymney valley in South Wales, Michael was the son of a butcher and enjoyed plenty of meat, a rarity in those days. So although he suffered a growth deformity which meant he never grew much beyond five feet and weighed well under eight stone, he was still very muscular and strong. Warburton, again with an eye for the publicity potential, inevitably came up with another nickname: 'The Mighty Midget'.

According to one report quoted by Les Woodland, Michael looked like a teenager well into his twenties: 'a childlike face topped a body lightly sloped forwards and always motionless; only his legs moved and turned madly at the greatest speeds.' In the early days he also raced with a toothpick in his mouth, which he claimed helped his breathing – but it became his trademark.

When he joined Aberaman CC Michael was taken under the wing of Arthur Linton, eight years his senior. As a grocer's assistant by this time, he had limited funds and so relied on goodwill from teammates. For important races Linton would lend him his bike.

Jimmy Michael won the Welsh championships at five miles and 50 miles on the Newport track when he was only seventeen. In June 1894 Linton encouraged Michael to race on the bigger stage and entered him for the Surrey 100 at Herne Hill. He didn't want Michael to make the same mistakes he had, so he organised an experienced pacing team led by his brothers Sam and Tom, and also ensured sufficient food.

Spectators mocked the boy lined up alongside the cream of British long-distance riders, but the derision was short-lived. He matched every attack from the gun, and after an hour was still among the leaders. By halfway he was in the lead, having lapped the field, and was just inside the record. He went on to see off all challengers and win with a seven-minute margin, in a new record time of 4 hours and 19 minutes. He was hailed by the press as 'the wonder boy from Wales'.

The man behind Linton and Michael was as famous as his riders, and is the subject of a probing book by historian Gerry Moore. Choppy Warburton was tall, handsome and loquacious. A sharp dresser and flamboyant personality, he sported luxuriant topcoats, flashy waistcoats, a lush handlebar moustache and a black bowler hat. In England, home of the 'gentleman amateur', he was loathed by authority – especially the National Cyclists' Union.

Warburton had been a successful athlete himself: a long-distance runner, in 1878 he was crowned amateur champion of England at four miles. One of the few working-class competitors to win an Amateur Athletic Club race, he was dubbed a 'plebian runner' for his trouble. During this period he worked as a warehouseman in the mills of his native Lancashire and despite working from 6am to 5.30pm for five-and-a-half days a week, he still managed to find time to train and compete at the highest level.

From his experience as a long-distance runner he developed a deep understanding of the importance of physical and mental preparation. He advocated specific training regimes to build endurance and stamina and also understood the value of recovery. He became a Svengali character, exercising complete control over his athletes (in the early days he also trained runners, rowers, boxers and even greyhounds). He was able to instil confidence and self-belief in his riders, all of whom improved under Warburton's guidance, in some cases becoming national and world champions.

Choppy never learned to ride a bike himself and was notoriously ignorant regarding the mechanics of bikes. In 1894 he was encouraged to ride tandem behind the French rider Albert Champion in a 2-kilometre race. Much to the amusement of the crowd he clung on to Champion for the duration, the duo wobbling to the finish line in last place!

He also spun his PR magic on himself: many of his methods were considered magical by the awestruck crowds. Since his early days Warburton had been secretive about his elaborate training and dietary methods, and also the contents of his ever-present, mysterious little black bottle. But far from concealing the bottle he would draw attention to himself at the trackside with his swirling overcoat, extravagant gestures and verbose rhetoric: all the showmanship of a magician. According to the *Paris-Vélo*:

> **"** He is everywhere at the same time, never in the same place. In the track centre he is the only one you see, his great overcoat and his derby hat pushed down to his ears with a bang of his fist. He gives out an air of mystery that intrigues rivals and thrills the public.
>
> From his pocket he suddenly takes out a glass container, shows it to his rider, uncorks it with dramatic care, pours the unknown mixture into a milk bottle and, still running, knocking over anyone who gets in his way, gets himself to the other side of the track to pass it to [his rider] …
>
> It's a drug, say some, just bluff say others; but drug or bluff, it's all the same. **"**

His bottle was variously reputed to contain simply water; a secret herbal mixture; or, more likely, performance-enhancing drugs – thought to be a cocktail of strychnine (to reinvigorate tired muscles), trimethyl (to ease pain and increase stamina) and heroin (to deaden the nerves). All three were known to be used in six-day racing where riders frequently hallucinated. In fact there is evidence that doping took place as early as the ancient Olympics.

Warburton's attitude towards drugs was not completely out of kilter with the times. Opium, laudanum, cocaine, morphine, arsenic, strychnine and nitroglycerine were all freely available in the 1890s. The pharmacist's only obligation in late Victorian England was to explain what each drug was supposed to be used for, but then anyone could buy and use them as they saw fit. Athletes were free to administer whatever substance they wanted and many took drugs; the authorities didn't issue a blacklist of banned substances and undertook no testing. The use of drugs was socially acceptable and even encouraged: Sherlock Holmes used cocaine and morphine to escape 'the dull routine of existence' between stimulating cases.

At this time Coca-Cola was marketed as a medicine – containing extracts of coca leaves, kola nuts and cocaine. It was immediately used by trainers as a stimulant for athletes. Cucca, a preparation that included cocaine, was even endorsed by the Cyclists' Touring Club. Manufacturers were aware of the value to racing cyclists and promoted relentlessly: Herne Hill's Cuca Cocoa Challenge Cup itself was the promotional vehicle for a company which claimed its products provided 'an extra kick'.

By 1894, with the cycling boom in full swing, crowds were flocking to the tracks. Once again Shorland won the Cuca Cocoa Cup, making it his own property with a ride of 460 miles 1,296 yards in 24 hours. (It was customary for riders who won three editions of a race to be given the trophy for keeps, rather than just for the year.) John Watts unearthed the reminiscences of H.W. Bartleet, a journalist who was there at the time, which were published in *Cycling* magazine many years later:

" Never shall I forget the excitement and display of mass enthusiasm. It was estimated that 20,000 people were packed around the track. But mere wooden gates were no bar to the thousands who had come to see the finish. They burst the barricades and squeezed in without paying. Hundreds over-ran the farm, then situated between the railway viaduct and the track, and clambered on the roofs of the farmer's sheds, some of which gave way. Shorland's last hour had been ridden to the accompaniment of one continuous roar of cheering, which never ceasing, followed him round and round the track. "

The following year, 1895, was the pinnacle of Warburton's success as a trainer and manager, with Jimmy Michael winning 22 out of the 28 races he rode, including the 100-kilometre paced event at the first ever professional world championship in August 1895 in Cologne, Germany.

The races were quite a spectacle, with each competitor being paced by seven men riding a quadruplet, followed by a triplet. The crowds expected the familiar format, where top riders controlled races until the final few laps and all hell broke loose with a frantic sprint finish. But in Cologne in 1895 all hell broke loose at the gun, when Michael attacked ferociously from the outset. He dominated from start to finish and crossed the line in 2 hours, 24 minutes – almost twelve laps ahead of his nearest rival, Rik Lutyen of Belgium.

Michael went on to reign supreme in paced racing from 1895 until 1899 and made a fortune as the biggest earner in cycling. But in 1896 he parted company with Warburton after yet another scandal. Michael was apparently so doped to the eyeballs at Catford in the Great Chain Match that he repeatedly fell off his bike – ultimately climbing back on to start cycling the wrong way around the track! Thousands of spectators were present at the high-profile meeting, screaming 'Dope!'

Nonetheless, there was huge demand and race organisers across Europe paid up to £200 to get him on the bill in front of up to 20,000 paying fans. He was even painted by Henri Toulouse-Lautrec for an advertising poster. By 1898 Michael had signed a contract for a series of ten races in the USA, guaranteeing him $2,500 per appearance. This was at a time when tradesmen would be lucky to earn £100 a year.

In an interview in the *New York Times*, quoted in Gerry Moore's book *The Little Black Bottle*, Michael described an average day:

" I get up in the morning between 7 and 8 o'clock. I breakfast on mutton chops, fruit and tea. I then take a good road ride, longer or shorter as my weight goes up or down. I dine at 1 o'clock in the afternoon. I have roast beef or mutton, tea and fruit. Never eat pastry. For supper my bill of fare is the same thing. My track work is done in the afternoon. I ride 10 or 15 miles at a good speed. I have no time to go round in the evenings. I don't go to afternoon teas and I have no time for society. I don't smoke. I don't drink. I take a glass of ale with my meals occasionally. I sleep about nine hours a day. "

Linton meanwhile jointly won the 1896 Bordeaux–Paris with Warburton's help, but paid the ultimate price. Again, drugs were involved. The Bordeaux–Paris race was one of Europe's Classic cycle races, and one of the longest and most gruelling, covering approximately 560 kilometres – more than twice the distance of most single-day races. It was unusual in that riders were paced behind cycles or tandems.

Linton started the race in a weakened state, due to his intense schedule of a long-distance race every week earlier in the season, and the race itself was pretty calamitous for Linton, with a series of crashes resulting in serious head wounds and other injuries. But according to *Sporting Life* he won with a little help from Warburton's little black bottle. In any event, the strain on his body took its toll: he finished the race looking like 'a corpse' as Choppy called him. He died nine weeks later, lacking the strength to battle against typhoid fever.

While 1896 was possibly the height of track cycling's popularity, not because of sheer numbers (which were actually significantly higher in the three decades that followed) but because of the sheer frenzy of excitement, the year represented the nadir of one of its most prominent characters. For some years Warburton had led the life of a top impresario, travelling first class, staying at the best hotels, wining and dining in the best restaurants and dressing in the latest fashions. He was famous, handsome and wealthy – and enjoyed the company of attractive women, to the detriment of his marriage and family life. But by now he had been variously accused of being a poisoner, a cheat and a charlatan. As Moore points out, Warburton admitted that 'races are not always ridden on the riders' merits'. The NCU banned him from appearing at any tracks in Britain and he had lost his two top riders. There is still no concrete evidence about his dubious 'methods', but the facts are that his riders usually burned bright and died young.

# From spectacle to sport

Just as rapidly as the craze had lit the public imagination, the late Victorian golden era for cycling began to lose its lustre. The cycle trade was in decline (latent demand had been quickly satisfied in the 1880s and 1890s, leaving too many manufacturers competing for dwindling sales) and the big firms no longer had money to sponsor pacing teams, professional riders or monster meetings.

Whereas the mid-1890s had witnessed huge crowds at London's eight or nine velodromes, numbers declined quickly towards the end of the century as new records were harder to beat and new sensations harder to find. And it was also a competitive arena: by the 1890s virtually every town in the UK had a track of some sort. Following Herne Hill's opening in spring 1891, the rival track in Putney had opened, swiftly followed by others in Canning Town, Westminster and Olympia.

By 1897 the owners had finally given up on the wooden track, which was slippery and dangerous when wet, replacing it with a cement surface, so when Crystal Palace track reopened the same year it meant there were three first-class velodromes within three or four miles of each other in south-east London. In 1895 a track had been built in Catford with seats for 1,000 spectators, a clubhouse and tennis courts. It had smooth concrete – an ideal surface for the new pump-up tyres. Despite the glamour and some superb meetings, such as the Chain Race, which saw American stars arriving by liner from New York, Catford lasted just five years. From its heyday in the 1880s when Catford CC was so successful that it had branches in Bristol, Cardiff, Nottingham and even Paris, and thousands of people turned up to watch races through Catford village (as it was in those days), by 1901 the track was gone and there were only 28 members left.

All track owners faced similar financial difficulties in the face of dwindling sponsorship and attendance revenue, but whereas most were able to sell the land when times were hard, the shareholders at Herne Hill were tenants of an estate strictly controlled by a charitable trust and, fortunately for the cycling community, were therefore forced to take a longer-term view.

Beyond the racetracks, upper- and middle-class recreational cycling was in decline as the wealthy were lured away by the car, and although bike prices were falling and the class structure in cycling clubs was changing, working-class cycling was not yet the mass phenomenon it would become by the 1920s. But working people certainly had more leisure, and for the first time an affordable means of personal transport to explore the countryside. Cycling clubs were as much about the social side as the sport, although they were complementary activities, with club runs being an essential prerequisite for race fitness.

During the late Victorian period competitive cycling had been controlled and organised for amateur sportsmen who generally came from the wealthy middle classes. When clubs or organisations held races there was enough money within the organising body to pay for prizes and expenses; the competitors only paid a nominal fee. The amateur ideal was zealously guarded, with a strict set of rules limiting prizes, advertising and sponsorship. On the Continent, on the other hand, amateurism was simply a stepping stone to a professional cycling career. But as the British cycling industry grew, increased investment and competition inevitably led to increased commercialisation of the racing scene. Money was now on offer.

During the early 1900s promoters also had the problem of unauthorised betting at meetings. As gambling was illegal, the onus was on organisers to prevent it, so it only tended to happen at the bigger meetings where their activities could be concealed by, and would benefit from, the large crowds. Herne Hill, like most velodromes, had bookmakers snaking through the crowds, doing business before disappearing again.

It had also long been normal to fix races: a group of riders would get together to arrange the result, use a third party to spread the betting among bookmakers, make a killing and share the spoils.

In the late 1890s talented working-class amateur riders saw the opportunity to improve their position in life by turning professional. Other sports such as bare-knuckle boxing and horse racing had accepted professionalism from the outset without question, but cycle racing was different. There was resistance from the old guard at the National Cyclists' Union, George Lacy Hillier and others, who still clung to the increasingly outmoded idea of 'gentleman amateurs' riding pure machines (in other words, no pneumatic tyres or safety bicycles). Professionalism and sponsorship of any sort was seen as a threat to the purity of the sport in England.

By the turn of the century a professional class had emerged nonetheless. Many riders remained amateurs (either by choice or limited ability), while many of the top racers took out professional licences. But this left a grey area in the middle. Riders who accepted bikes and equipment, or appeared to endorse or advertise gear, were known as a 'maker's amateur'. They were generally up-and-coming young riders, without the independent finances of 'gentleman amateurs'; they were loftily referred to as 'colliers' and butchers' boys'. Not technically professionals, but not strictly amateur either. In France they were known as 'independents'. They could win money and wear advertising, and ride against amateurs and professionals as they wished – but not both at the same time (because amateurs were forbidden to ride with professionals).

Leading manufacturers like Dunlop and Gladiator had teams of up to 60 pacers to support the star riders, sponsored by cycle-makers like Humber, Rudge and Swift, who brought fast and exciting racing, and capacity crowds. In the early years, most records and many races were paced. Initially this was human-powered pacing, eventually using teams of riders on five-person tandems, changing over to sustain high speeds. But in the pursuit for ever-faster speeds and thrilling races, human pacers were replaced by motorcycles. For a short period in the late 1890s and early 20th century, cycle racing behind pacers was the most popular form of public entertainment. The racers were highly paid celebrity stars, with hordes of fans following their lives through the press.

Thousands of people paid to watch multi-manned or motorised pacing machines thundering around Herne Hill and other tracks across Europe and the United States, dragging racers in their wake. They were the fastest men on earth and it spelled danger. There were as many as six teams on the track at any time. Crashes were frequent and spectacular, often serious – and occasionally fatal.

The huge motorcycles roared around the track, often without silencers and with flames flaring from the exhaust stub. They had a roller on a frame at the rear to create a uniform distance to the cyclist and avoid crashes caused by the rider touching the back of the motorbike, but there were few other regulations. The drivers stood or sat bolt upright to offer the maximum windbreak, and the handlebars were extended to facilitate this position.

The cyclists tucked themselves tightly behind the pacers on specially designed bikes made to handle the high speed and to get them as close as possible to the rear of the motorcycle:

including reversed front forks and a smaller front wheel to let the stayer bend forward into the slipstream. The pacers wore leather coats, goggles, and leather and steel helmets, but many racers simply wore a flat cap and regular club kit.

By the early 1900s racers were hitting speeds of 55mph and by the 1920s they were doing over 75mph. At high speed, a burst tyre or broken bike often proved fatal. In their pursuit of speed, records, money and fame, many died when they came crashing down on the track, or went flying up and over the banking into the grandstand of spectators. A crash in Berlin in July 1909 killed nine when a motorcycle went into the stands and exploded.

St John Ambulance became a regular feature of track racing, according to John Watts. 'The appearance of this excellent corps has a slightly lugubrious effect on racing men and spectators alike,' reported *Cycling*, 'but in these days of terrible speeds, crowded tracks and incompetent riders of safety cycles with weak forks and wobbling course, they are becoming more and more a painful necessity.'

In 1902, during a race on a steeply banked wooden track in Berlin, Jimmy Michael crashed. Having done 57 miles at an average speed of nearly 60mph, the rear wheel of the motorbike in front of him collapsed. He fractured his skull and suffered multiple injuries and was never the same rider again. Riders like Michael and Arthur Linton could earn big money, but had to ride incredibly hard to do so.

The bunch road races that had terrorised the countryside in the 1880s had all but died out by this time, but their absence concealed another story that marked a turning point in the history of British cycling. Not all of these cyclists had forsaken the road for the track by any means.

Back in 1888 the National Cyclists' Union asked clubs to restrict races to closed tracks, which in part had contributed to the explosion in track cycling, but it was not to everyone's taste. Road racers could see they needed a different approach in order to stay on the road and could no longer charge about in bunch races, but within months a rebel organisation had been launched encouraging riders to continue competing on the roads, albeit in a different style of race: the eccentric and secretive sport of time trialling.

The rebels' opening meeting, involving eleven clubs, was organised by Frederick Thomas 'Biddy' Bidlake, who is often credited with being the father of formalised time trialling. Although Bidlake was ultimately remembered as one of the most significant administrators of British cycle racing, he also broke countless road and track records on his favoured tricycle. His record of 410 miles 1,110 yards set up in the 24-hour Cuca Cup race in 1893 at Herne Hill still stood at the date of his death, 40 years later. The Road Records Committee (quickly renamed the Road Records Association, and later still the Road Time Trials Council, RTTC) simply adopted the NCU's records as its own and carried on where the now-rival organisation had left off.

In contrast with the chaos and showmanship of mass road

racing, time trialling was all about individual performance. Time trials are simple: riders set off at 1-minute intervals and race a set distance against the clock. Each rider competes individually, and the one who completes the distance in the shortest time wins. If a rider is caught by the one behind, he has to drop back so there is no slip-streaming, pacing or bunch racing.

Often called 'the race of truth', time trials are considered the purest form of cycling by many, with little opportunity for tactics: the strongest rider usually wins. It's a mathematical sport, requiring lots of decisions about gearing and pacing, with the cyclists aiming to cross the line without an ounce of energy left. It requires obsessive focus, rhythm and concentration. Conversely it has none of the random chance factors associated with racing as part of a peloton.

Staggered starts meant that those competing could claim to be just 'going about their business'. Races took place early in the morning on isolated roads deep in the countryside. The cycling press were asked not to print dates, venues, start times or results of races. Secrecy was maintained by providing the location and timing of the races in code: referencing courses such as G10 or Q19 and dates such as 'weekend 13'. Lists of riders were headed 'Private and confidential'. Competitors dressed from head to toe in black (with tights and alpaca jackets) without numbers or identification to make them as 'inconspicuous' as possible.

The first race under these rules was over 50 miles and organised by the North Road Cycling Club in October 1895, although time trials had been held before. Trials settled into five formats: 25-, 50- and 100-mile courses, plus races to see how many miles could be covered in twelve and 24 hours.

This emergency stop-gap race format was to dominate British road racing for the foreseeable future. With one mis-guided gesture, which became a defining moment in the history of British cycle racing, the conservatively minded National Cyclists' Union kick-started a division between the two branches of the sport that would last for 50 years. This rivalry effectively cut off British cycling from the develop-ment of road racing in continental Europe until the end of the Second World War. It was the reason road cycling did not become a mass spectator sport in Britain as it did on the Continent.

Cycle racing in Europe was developing in a completely different direction. Road racing flourished: one-day Classics such as Liège–Bastogne–Liège and Paris–Roubaix started in the last decade of the 19th century. The Tour de France started in 1903 and the Giro d'Italia in 1909. Whole com-munities would turn out to watch hugely popular pelotons storming through the countryside in a festival of colour, exu-berance and noise, while their British neighbours raced alone at dawn, dressed in black.

Although British riders had won many of these early European races – James Moore winning Paris–Rouen in 1869, George Pilkington Mills winning the first Bordeaux–Paris in 1891 and then Arthur Linton in 1896 – that dominance soon faded. In fact it would take another 65 years for a Brit to win a Classic, Tom Simpson triumphing in the Tour of Flanders, one of the five 'Monuments', in 1961.

❋

British racers that turned to the track rather than trying their hand at time trialling, became some of the best riders in the world because of this specialisation. An active and highly competitive track racing scene during the early years of the new century was producing world-beaters. Amateur track racing went through one of its most successful phases ever.

Between 1900 and 1914 a total of fourteen world championship titles were brought home to Britain, with Leon Meredith and sprinters Vic Johnson, Bill Bailey, A.L. Reed and J.S. Benyon all racing regularly at Herne Hill. Meredith and Johnson had both enjoyed further success since the inaugural Good Friday Meeting. At Herne Hill, Meredith dominated the Penrose Cup for the always popular 10-mile point-to-point race, winning three years on the trot from 1907 to 1909, earning the right to keep the trophy. On one memorable day in September 1909, Vic Johnson set three world records at Herne Hill for unpaced standing-start quarter-mile, three-quarter-mile and one mile. His quarter-mile time (28 seconds) stood as the world record for 21 years and as the British amateur record for nearly 40 years.

Bill Bailey was born in Mayfair, the son of a domestic coachman, and went on to become the dominant amateur sprinter in the period before the First World War. He won four world championship gold medals between 1909 and 1913 before turning professional in 1914, but the war robbed him of his best years. There wouldn't be another sprinter like him, or a golden era like this, until Reg Harris emerged just after the Second World War. Bailey was part of a particularly memorable race in 1911 at Herne Hill when he defeated past and future champions Vic Johnson and Thomas 'Tiny' Johnson (no relation) in the 550-yard scratch race – the simplest of all races, where riders compete over a set distance and the first over the line wins.

With light brown wavy hair, a boyish face and rippling physique, Bailey attracted crowds of adoring fans on his many tours of Europe, Australia, and the United States. He won so regularly in the USA that his American fans at Madison Square Garden would affectionately subvert the jazz standard 'Bill Bailey, Won't You Please Come Home?', imploring him to 'go home'.

As well as victory in the world championships, the three Olympic Games between 1900 and 1908 resulted in British riders winning nine gold medals. When the Games first came to London in 1908, it was a gold rush for British cycling. Great Britain won five of the six gold medals awarded, plus three silver and one bronze – fully nine of the eighteen medals up for grabs! But for some bad luck, the tally could have been even higher.

The Olympic cycling was all held on the 660-yard track at White City Stadium in Shepherd's Bush, which had been specially built for the Games and could accommodate 60,000 spectators – the largest stadium in the world at the time. The cycling competition was held during mid-July, when *Sporting Life* noted: 'the weather was the reverse of pleasant. As a matter of fact, it was the rule rather than the exception for the track to be flooded.'

The first event was the 20-kilometre race on 14 July. Meredith, the greatest British long-distance track racer of this era was expected to win, but he didn't fare well at the 1908 Olympics. In the final he punctured early and lost two laps before remounting, too late to make an impact on the race. Clarence Kingsbury, a 25-year-old from Portsmouth, went on to win. A versatile rider, he won NCU titles every year from 1907 to 1912 at distances between 440 yards and 50 miles. Benjamin Jones, also of Great Britain, took silver, with the bronze going to Joseph Werbrouck of Belgium.

In the 660-yard sprint final Karl Neumer of Germany jumped after one-third of a lap, gaining six lengths quickly. Just before the straight, Vic Johnson and Frenchman Emile Demangel caught him and battled to the finish with Johnson winning by inches.

The French pair of Maurice Schilles and André Auffray were both top sprinters individually, but they had never ridden together as a tandem prior to the 2-kilometre event at these Games. The final was a slow race, but the French tandem gradually drew away in the straight to win easily. Great Britain won both silver (Frederick Hamlin and Thomas 'Tiny' Johnson) and bronze (Charles Brooks and Walter Isaacs).

No medals were awarded in the 1,000-metre sprint because the time limit was exceeded in the final held on

16 July, making the race void. 'This was a fiasco,' claimed *Sporting Life*, as quoted by Bill Mallon in his book on the 1908 Games,

> for not only was the race declared void through the time limit being exceeded, but, in addition, Kingsbury and Vic Johnson punctured. The former was thrown out of the race before half a lap had been covered, and Johnson's mishap occurred at the beginning of the last banking. Most of the work was done on the banks at a crawl, but in spite of the red flag being shown the competitors, they continued at the same rate of progression. They were hopelessly outside the time limit when the sprint came, when, with Johnson puncturing, Schilles and Jones rode out an inches finish. The Frenchman got there by two or three inches.

This was the first time that a team pursuit race was contested at the Olympics. Britain won comfortably, led by Meredith, with Benjamin Jones, Ernest Payne and Clarence Kingsbury (who won his second gold).

There were two great races on 18 July, the final day. At the bell in the 5,000 metres race, the Dutchman Gerard Bosch van Drakestein jumped the field and was not caught until the final straight. Benjamin Jones then passed him, taking a length's lead. But the Frenchmen Schilles and Auffray were in hot pursuit and only failed by inches to catch Jones on the line. This was Jones' second gold medal of the Olympics, to add to his silver, earning the Wigan-born collier the most impressive British Olympic medal haul until Chris Hoy's Beijing performance.

The 100-kilometre race was considered the major event of the cycling programme, with a cup donated by the Prince of Wales for the winner. Leon Meredith was of course the hot favourite, but once again fell victim to bad luck – he was involved in a crash early on and although he remounted, he never really recovered. At 70 kilometres Charles Bartlett punctured, but was paced back on to the pack in eight laps by Canadian Harry Young. The final lap came down to four riders: Bartlett, Charles Denny, Octave Lapize and William Pett. Three Britons and a Frenchman. The Brits paced the quick-sprinting Bartlett, leading him out for the final sprint, which he won by a wheel. Denny took silver and Lapize won bronze. The Frenchman, incidentally, went on to win the Tour de France in 1910, and remains the only rider to win the Paris–Roubaix for three consecutive years (1909–11).

As dominant as Great Britain was as a cycling nation in 1908, these were their last individual track cycling gold medals for more than 80 years – until Chris Boardman's 1992 victory in Barcelona, which opened the floodgates once again.

In September 1908 the National Cyclists' Union promoted their first Meeting of Champions at Herne Hill: an event that would showcase the very best national and international riders for the next half-century. They aimed to get as many track champions as possible together at the end of the season – a popular and long-lasting formula. Like the Good Friday Meetings that opened the season, the Meeting of Champions could usually be guaranteed to close it with a full house.

❋

The flourishing period of good fortune and prosperity in Edwardian England augured well for cycling as pastime and sport, but the war put paid to that. Race meetings continued throughout the war, but they were modest and subdued affairs. Intense patriotic fervour in the early days of the conflict created a climate that discouraged enjoyment of sport as either competitor or spectator, and cycling was at best seen as a tolerable way to 'recharge the batteries' while focusing on the war effort. Few people went against the spirit of the age, and track cycling became almost non-existent. Conscription and casualties soon claimed the majority of active racing men anyway.

These were extraordinary times. Crystal Palace FC played their Southern League fixtures at Herne Hill stadium from February 1915 through to the end of the season owing to their ground being requisitioned for use by the military. From 1916 entry to races was restricted exclusively to members of His Majesty's Forces in an attempt to placate public opinion and any profits were donated to Lord Kitchener's Fund for soldiers at the front. Similar meetings were held at tracks around the country, organised by Leon Meredith in aid of the Cyclists' Prisoner of War Fund.

The 1917 Good Friday Meeting was promoted as United Services Sports and also included athletics and other entertainments. There was a 'novelty race': a match between Mrs Andrews, a well-known rider, and 'an unknown lady' (women's races were still considered a novelty, and some riders were not prepared to reveal their identities in the programmes due to the social stigma). The anonymous racer won the one-lap pursuit by two seconds, then Mrs Andrews won the scratch by inches.

But a more pernicious stigma persisted beyond the war years. Again according to John Watts' research, G. Wilson Smith, who took over as General Secretary of the Southern Counties Cycling Union under acrimonious circumstances in 1923, dismissed the wartime efforts of the Good Friday Meeting organiser, saying: 'I'm sorry Mr Stapley could find no better occupation in the years 1915–19 as did most of us.'

# 5

## Racing at the Mecca

The first post-war Good Friday Meeting in 1919, promoted as The Victory Meeting, was hailed by *Cycling* as 'Herne Hill's Revival' and brought in a crowd of nearly 8,000. The quality of racing was still poor following the lack of competitive racing during the war, but that soon changed. And memories of the pre-war success of British riders gradually brought back the crowds.

Such was the split personality of the British cycling fraternity that during the inter-war years racers still had to make a choice: down one path lay the introverted and clandestine, cult-like world of time trials; down the other was the extrovert and colourful track racing scene. At Herne Hill, world champions performed at what was now unequivocally the country's premier racetrack throughout the 1920s and 1930s, regularly attracting attendances of 10,000 or more.

A trip to the velodrome used to be a social occasion. People would come along to the track to meet their friends: some had a favourite spot to meet; others just circulated.

Top hats and greatcoats had been replaced by fedoras and woollen suits. On the track, woollen kit was still the norm, but more riders were wearing leather hairnets (helmets), especially in motor-paced races. The steel bikes were also much as they had been since the advent of the safety cycle, with flared drop handlebars.

Track riders rode their bikes to and from races. Punctures were common so they would fold and pack spare tyres under the saddle or on the handlebars, or wear them looped and knotted around their shoulders – like the Tour de France riders of the time. Wealthier riders would carry light race wheels attached to detachable mounts bolted to the front forks.

Given that time trialling existed in a vacuum, effectively cut off from Continental cycling, track racing was the only branch of the sport in which British cyclists could hope to measure themselves against international opposition. British track racers competed internationally through the 1920s, 1930s and 1940s without the disadvantages experienced by their road racing counterparts.

Track racing enjoyed considerable support across the country through the inter-war years, with stars in the likes of Albert White and Albert Theaker from Lincolnshire, Syd Cozens and Jack Sibbit from Manchester, the four Wyld brothers from Derbyshire, the Horn brothers from Norfolk and London riders Frank Southall and Thomas 'Tiny' Johnson (the diminutive rider from Fulham built on his 1908 silver medal with two more in the individual sprint and team pursuit at the 1920 Olympics in Antwerp and the world amateur sprint title in 1922). They were joined at Herne Hill by the cream of continental European racers from this era, including Jef Scherens, Jacques van Egmond, Toni Merkens and Louis Gérardin.

Racing was taking place at other venues across London such as the one at Paddington, the leading west London ground, but that track was in a public park so promoters could only charge for admission to the centre, leaving Herne Hill as the only one where organisers could viably charge admission. South London was therefore the main place where Londoners could see the cream of British cyclists and champions from overseas; Herne Hill cemented its place at the centre of track racing in Britain. Promoters could be assured of a full house for many top-class events; and Saturday meetings, and even weekday evening meetings, would frequently attract several thousand spectators.

Sprint matches between the world's best professionals were now an established feature of the Good Friday Meetings. Bill Bailey made his first appearance as a professional in 1921 when he defeated Marcel Duputy, the European champion, in a series of sprint matches.

Herbert Goodwin, a new breed of unashamedly professional promoter, unlike the strictly amateur George Lacy Hillier and his colleagues, organised the 1923 Good Friday Meeting which attracted a record attendance of 13,000. Bailey was there again, taking on the US champion Willie Spencer and French champion Paul Didier. Spencer won two rounds, to Bailey's one. But Tiny Johnson, by now world champion, was on great form, winning the 550-yard scratch and the De Frece point-to-point.

Always the showman, Goodwin's meetings usually included a 'novelty event' or prize-giving by popular sports-people or entertainers of the day. Rochdale-born actress and singer Gracie Fields was at several, and even brought a chorus of showgirls to compete in a cycle race. Following special coaching, the girls apparently rode well. Goodwin also organ-ised publicity events in conjunction with the Lyons Corner House restaurant and tea shop chain. The waitresses, popu-larly known as 'nippies', raced in their billowing black linen uniforms, with starched white collars and cuffs, and lace caps. Shorts were the only compromise for modesty's sake.

That said, Goodwin was one of the few promoters to encourage genuine women's track racing during the 1920s and 1930s, often putting on women's events in the same pro-gramme as top international stars, according to John Watts – something that wasn't universally applauded, as *Cycling* magazine's reporter whinged: 'If any criticism can be made about Saturday's fare it was on this score – that there was a little too much to be seen, in more than one respect, of the ladies.' But Goodwin's events were primarily successful because of the quality of the racers and racing, rather than the gimmicks.

The early 1920s also saw the emergence of a new breed of trainer, with initial forays into analytical training (an approach that would be taken to the nth degree for Team GB in the

21st century under Peter Keen) and one of the most successful proponents was Sam Mussabini, a London-born athletics and cycling coach who lived at 84 Burbage Road from 1913 until his death in 1927 – an address chosen because the billiard room led onto the garden, which had direct access to the grounds of Herne Hill stadium.

Mussabini bought a cine camera to record the men he was coaching, to ensure posture and movement patterns were correct. He coached the Polytechnic Cycling Club in London, as well as the Dunlop Tyre Company's riders, with great success and enjoyed a strong reputation. He is perhaps most famous, however, for his record with his athletes in the 1920 and 1924 Olympics, with the latter group being the inspiration for the film *Chariots of Fire*.

1924 saw the emergence of Harry Wyld in the 5-mile De Frece Cup at Herne Hill. The 24-year-old rider broke clear after only five laps and by the thirteenth had lapped the field. This was the start of a series of victories that made the burly Wyld a firm favourite with crowds. He won the cup outright after two more wins and when West End musical impresario Sir Walter de Frece sponsored another cup, he took that trophy home to Derby too.

Wyld went on to win bronze medals at the 1924 Olympics in Paris for the 50-kilometre track race and at the 1928 Olympics in Amsterdam for the 4,000-metre team pursuit with his brothers Percy and Arthur, and George 'Monty' Southall, brother of Frank. They actually recorded the two fastest times of the tournament, including a new Olympic record in the quarter-final (although it was a brief moment of joy: the record was broken again the next day). It was all the more amazing that there was yet another, older, prize-winning brother, Ralph, with whom they formed an invincible team pursuit family.

The 1924 Good Friday Meeting also had a memorable 2,000-metre tandem handicap when R. Austin and E. Burgess went over the banking and landed in the crowd with their tandem.

In 1927 Harry Wyld's run of De Frece Cup wins came to an end when he faced Frank Southall, the leading road time trial rider in the country, a local to Herne Hill and member of Norwood Paragon CC, who tried his hand on the track in a series of highly popular races against Wyld.

Southall made his name at Herne Hill as a 20-year-old in May 1925 when he attacked the national hour record. A blustery wind was blowing across the track on the night, making the attempt even more difficult. But after the first mile Southall was up on the record by almost six seconds and he increased his lead every mile, finally passing the old record with almost two minutes in hand. In the remaining time he added another two and a half laps to break the record with 25 miles 1,520 yards.

His entry in the *Golden Book of Cycling* in 1932 read:

> " Southall holds the world's unpaced standing start track records at one, five, ten and twenty miles. He holds 28 national track records. On the road

> he has won every classic open event, including
> hill-climbs, making competition records at 25, 50 and
> 100 miles. "

He won the silver medal in the individual road race at the 1928 Olympics in Amsterdam and would have won gold if a protest had been upheld, that winner Harry Hansen of Denmark had cut the course. In the 1932 Los Angeles Olympics he took team pursuit bronze, with William Harvell, Ernest Johnson and Charles Holland. He turned professional in 1934 and spent the rest of his racing career breaking more records.

He also appeared in the 1932 Olympic road race, but only came sixth. This was the last Olympic road race to be run as a time trial; the change to massed start from 1936 committed Britain to the international road racing wilderness. According to Les Woodland, *Cycling* magazine saw anything other than time trialling and track racing as almost corrupt, and complained: 'The Olympic Games were the last stronghold of the genuine international trial of road riding ability, free from tactics or bunching.'

Southall's early days were spent on the road after bursting on to the scene at Norwood Paragon as an eighteen-year-old in 1922, and his only experience on the track was in pursuits or record attempts, rather than bunch races, and consequently bookmakers offered odds of 10-1 for his first ever track race at the 1927 Good Friday Meeting. Many of the locals were tempted to wager on their idol: what he lacked in experience he made up for in speed.

Southall was competing in the De Frece Cup, a 5-mile point-to-point race, in which the normal tactic is to sprint for the line in each points lap, then ease off while everyone recovers before the next sprint. Southall wasn't a great sprinter, so when everyone eased up after the first lap he simply carried on. He maintained a punishingly fast pace, meaning few riders could hold his wheel (Harry Wyld being the exception, of course) and he completely nullified the sprinters, eventually winning by one point.

The battles between Southall and the Wyld brothers continued throughout the late 1920s. Harry Wyld's track experience led him to many victories, but Southall reigned at unpaced riding and pursuit races. One frustrating team pursuit against the Wylds in 1928 saw his team fall apart every time he was at the front because they simply couldn't hold his wheel.

One particular 50-mile tandem-paced duel between Southall and Wyld at Herne Hill in September 1928 went down in folklore, with the two riders pushing each other on to break record after record after record. Wyld led from the start and broke the 2-mile intermediate record that had stood since 1904 – with another 48 miles still to go! He kept Southall at bay until 28 miles, then the lead began to change repeatedly. Southall broke the 30 miles record, Wyld got the 31 miles record, Southall took each record at 32–35 miles, Wyld took it back to break records at 36–38, before Southall came back yet again to take the 39–43-mile records! Wyld then made a decisive counter-attack to take the remaining miles, eventually finishing in a record 50-mile time of 1 hour and 39 minutes, with Southall fading at almost 2 minutes behind.

One of the most popular races in the 1930s was the Australian pursuit, in which riders would set off at intervals around the track and when one rider caught another, that rider would be eliminated from the race, until, after a set period of time, the bunch of remaining riders would sprint for the line. This race format was dominated in the early years by Southall. In 1930 he eliminated five of his seven opponents before the 10 minutes had elapsed; the following year he cleared the track of competitors in just over nine minutes.

The huge attendances of over 10,000 spectators in the early to mid-1920s declined later in the decade and even more so into the early 1930s as the great depression hit, with hardship and unemployment widespread. The quality of the competitive racing remained undiminished, however, and by the mid-1930s some wealth and confidence had recovered and people had more money to spend on leisure activities again.

In September 1936, six-day racing returned to London, having died out in Britain in the early years of the 20th century. American promoters had taken to the idea in the 1890s, when 'sixes' were established as endurance events in which racers had to do lap after lap for twelve, then eighteen, and ultimately 24 hours a day, with only brief rests for sleep and massage. These grimly watchable events proved as popular in the US – attracting huge crowds to the old Madison Square Garden, which established itself as a regular venue – as they had to Victorian Londoners.

Public opinion turned against the extreme cruelty after a few years and in 1899 two-man teams were introduced in races at Madison Square Garden, so that riders could rest while their partners took a turn. At the end of one rider's turn, their partner would be launched into the action with a shove or 'hand-sling'. This is basically the 'Madison' tag-race style that we still know today, which caught on and spread to Europe. Over the years the brutal hours of endurance also lessened, while more variety and change of pace was introduced to the programme.

The race at the Empire Pool building in Wembley in 1936, on a steeply banked track built especially for the occasion, saw this new style Madison-based six-day racing witnessed by an incredible 80,000 people. In turn the long-standing owners of Herne Hill – the Peacock family – were encouraged to plan a covered stand to seat 7,000 – although despite their optimism the building never materialised.

Two leading riders in the 1930s were from yet another cycling dynasty: the Horns. Dennis Horn was probably Britain's most successful track rider through the 1930s, but his brother Cyril was also a brilliant all-rounder. During the 1930s, rural Fenland-born Dennis and Cyril graduated from the rough-and-tumble grass-track racing at county fairs to the heights of British cycling at Herne Hill, becoming national stars in the process.

Dennis's story is told in a biography by Peter Underwood. He was an immensely powerful rider, capable of pushing gears as high as 96 inches, typically in extended high-speed sprint finishes to events of all distances. He was younger than Cyril by five years and followed his brother into competitive ice-skating and cycling (a popular combination of sports at the time, and one which is still common in Belgium and the Netherlands today). But whereas Cyril remained the stronger skater, Dennis was the more successful on the track once he had learned the craft. Cyril was one of the top sprinters in the country, but Dennis nearly always had the edge.

In September 1929 they appeared at a major hard track meeting for the first time: the national 5-mile championship at Herne Hill, although neither reached the final. But by the start of the summer track season of 1932 Dennis had established himself as a nationally recognised rider on grass and hard track and was rapidly becoming one of the stars of British track racing.

The brothers typically started their training slowly, Dennis only began seriously in February and would test himself in local 25-mile time trials, before launching his season at the Good Friday Meeting. But he rarely did well there.

Dennis was paired with Jack Sibbit in the Olympic tandem trials at Herne Hill in April 1932 – and won, but Dennis wasn't prepared to spend six weeks in the United States when there were cups to be won back home. Two days later they won the national one-mile tandem championship at Herne Hill in dominant fashion, but it wasn't enough to change Dennis's mind. Valuable trophies were won outright after three victories and Horn wasn't the only rider to turn down offers to compete in the Olympics or world championships if they clashed with a potentially lucrative third win.

The rules of amateurism were still very strict in this period and the merest hint of cash prizes could result in a suspension. Nonetheless there were plenty of ways to circumvent these rules. In the early 1930s common prizes included canteens of cutlery and watches, or a joint of meat or string of sausages from the local butchers, through to grandfather clocks. In rural areas the prize may have been a bag of potatoes or a runt pig. No money was directly offered, although there was always a corner of the track where riders could sell their winnings for hard cash. Pawn shops across the country did brisk trade every Monday morning through the summer, exchanging prizes for cash.

Sibbit and Horn were both in excellent form on the tandem, but that didn't prevent an intense rivalry as individuals. Sibbit, from the Manchester Wheelers' Club, had won a silver medal at the 1928 Olympics in Amsterdam riding with Ernie Chambers (Sibbit rode on the front, Chambers was his stoker) and by 1936 he had held twelve national titles, including tandem sprints. He was a lean, dark-haired man who often raced in a black vest. The 1,000-yard national sprint championship had been introduced in 1930, and having won it in 1931, Sibbit was hotly tipped to do so again in 1932, at Herne Hill.

The deciding race was between Horn, Sibbit, and Sibbit's other tandem partner, Chambers. Horn was winning, but looked to his left and swerved right, forcing Sibbit up the banking. Although this meant Horn would be disqualified for not holding his line, Sibbit took no chances, grabbing hold of his younger rival's seat post while he sprinted past to take first place.

As the 1930s moved on from the initial years of depression, large crowds were enjoying the cream of international track racing at Herne Hill. In 1933 the reigning Olympic sprint champion Jacques van Egmond of Holland and German champion Toni Merkens were brought in to race against top British amateurs.

In a series of match sprints with Dennis Horn and Jack Sibbit, Merkens proved the best sprinter. The same riders met in the 550-yard scratch race and on that occasion Horn got the better of Merkens. In the final event of the day, the Palmer Cup 5-mile point-to-point, Merkens won again. By this time he was one of the most popular riders on British tracks, and he returned the following year to do even better, winning the 550-yard scratch against sixteen of Britain's best sprinters, international sprint matches against Dennis Horn and also the Palmer Cup again.

The Paragon 5-mile Club Championship in 1933 also went down in history. Nine men were still fighting for victory at the bell, when two of the leading riders touched wheels and fell, with the rest of the field ploughing into the carnage; one rider went over the rails (a not infrequent occurrence at the time). A few escaped injury, the rest went to nearby King's College Hospital and the race was abandoned. In future years the race was listed in event programmes as the 'Bloodbath Five'.

Merkens won the Palmer Cup a further time in 1935 to make the trophy his own property. That year also saw an omnium between two of the world's top professionals: Belgian Karel Kaers and Frenchman Maurice Richard. In 1934 Kaers had become the youngest world road champion at only 20, when riding the race for the first time. He also went on to win the Tour of Flanders in 1939. Richard meanwhile was holder of the world hour record.

Then in 1937 there was a contest between three of Europe's top sprinters. First, there was the phenomenal Jef Scherens from Belgium, with blond hair and a wide smile, who won the world professional sprint championship seven times: every year between 1932 and 1937, and then again after the war in 1947.

Secondly, Albert Richter: a three-time winner of the Paris Grand Prix, amateur world champion in 1932 and seven-time champion of Germany. He was on the podium of every world championship from 1933 to 1939, although he never won the gold medal – which usually went to the unassailable Scherens. He was a tall and handsome athlete with blond hair and blue eyes – and also a vocal anti-fascist. He emigrated to Paris in 1933 to escape the growth of Nazism, but returned regularly to race. He stayed loyal to his Jewish coach who remained in Germany, sending him winnings from races when he was prohibited from coaching. He often stood alone in refusing to make the Nazi salute on the podium and after one meeting in Berlin, on New Year's Eve 1939 he was taken from a train by the Gestapo and killed. He had been smuggling money for Jews in his bicycle tyres.

But back at Herne Hill in 1937, there was also Louis Gérardin, reigning French sprint champion, who went on to win the title thirteen times in his career, as well as silver medals in two world championships. He was also later the lover of Edith Piaf, of whom he said, 'Forty-eight hours with Piaf are more tiring than a lap in the Tour de France'.

Despite coming directly from a winter season on the indoor tracks of continental Europe, the riders thrilled the Herne Hill crowds, even overcoming spring snowfall which threatened the meeting with cancellation.

Merkens and Horn rode many hotly contested races during this period, and Horn went on to describe the German as his only real friend in the world of cycling. Many people believed Horn to be the equal of any amateur sprint cyclist in the world, so it's a shame that he never took the opportunity to compete on an Olympic stage. He missed the 1936 Olympics in Berlin for the same reason he'd missed the 1932 Games in Los Angeles: 'I couldn't afford to go,' he said many years later, 'because I'd got several cups I wanted to win.' He simply couldn't live by the National Cyclists' Union's strict rules of amateurism, which meant he needed to choose between a month in Germany without income or picking up prizes back home. In Berlin, the sprint gold was won by Merkens, leaving Britain with a solitary bronze medal in the team pursuit.

Tandem pursuits were also heavily featured at Herne Hill around this time, usually between four pairs. In 1936 Ernie Mills and Bill Paul set a tandem world hour record of 30 miles and 793 yards. In the 1937 Good Friday Meeting they cleared the track of all rivals in just under four minutes in what should have been a 10-minute pursuit. They were both popular local riders and members of the Addiscombe Cycle Club in Croydon, regularly racing at Herne Hill throughout the 1930s.

Later that year Mills and Paul visited the newly built Velodromo Vigorelli in Milan to attempt the world record. Built in 1935, it was a new model for velodromes, with a fast board surface, steep banking (45 degrees, compared to Herne Hill's 12 degrees) and covered stands to seat 30,000 spectators. It rapidly became a favourite venue for record attempts and world championships, earning a reputation as the world's fastest track that lasted until the late 1960s. Mills and Paul successfully rode a world record distance for the hour, that stood until September 2000 when it was beaten at Manchester Velodrome.

The so-called Monday 'comp' started in 1936 as a sprint competition held on Monday evenings. The best racers would ride the 'Star' events and the rest would ride in the

'Medal' category. After winning 10 points a medal rider would win promotion to the star event, all leading towards a gala end-of-season finale. After the war it was extended to include distance races in the programme and carried on through to the 1990s.

Good Friday, meanwhile, had become an important fixture in the international cycling calendar. Big names in the cycle industry, such as Dunlop and BSA, were also starting to take an interest in racing as a means of exposure for the company and donated valuable trophies for competition. A meeting in 1938 sponsored by Dunlop to celebrate the 50th anniversary of the pneumatic tyre attracted a stellar line-up of racers and a capacity crowd.

Things were looking positive for cycling, but once again war intervened. Two days after the German invasion of Poland on 1 September 1939, Britain declared war on Germany, and within a month Herne Hill stadium was being used as an anti-aircraft and barrage balloon site, the track suddenly out of bounds.

The general attitude towards recreational sport during wartime was more relaxed in the Second World War than during the First World War, however: race meetings continued elsewhere into 1940, mainly to raise money for the War Funds to supply troops overseas. Despite the lack of international riders, they were still testament to the wartime spirit.

The Good Friday Meeting planned for 1940 couldn't take place at Herne Hill, so it was held in London's only other velodrome at the time, Paddington, and the proceeds were donated to the Red Cross Fund. The 1941 meeting was cancelled as the Germans continued to bomb London heavily, but by the summer the German offensive was focused on the Russian front and air raids were less intense, so the site was handed back.

The lease was due for renewal in March 1942, but after 50 years' family ownership the son of one of the original Peacock brothers didn't want to continue and following negotiations it was taken over by the National Cyclists' Union. But three years of neglect had left the track in a state of disrepair with weeds and small trees growing through cracks. A clean-up took place in autumn 1942 under the direction of Alfred Willett (who remarkably had been the groundsman since 1893!), with four farm workers using scythes. But the track was fundamentally damaged and in need of resurfacing, something which wouldn't happen quickly during wartime.

Herne Hill was not alone being in such a state after the privations of war. The concrete surface of Oerlikon Velodrome in Zurich, which hosted the 1946 world championships, was apparently so appalling that bikes were difficult to control. Henri Lemoine, the French rider who enjoyed a 30-year career as a professional cyclist specialising in motor-paced racing, reportedly had a loin of beef sewn into his shorts to cushion his derrière from the blows.

Work on Herne Hill was finally completed in the summer of 1944, and after the reopening was delayed by various problems, including a flying bomb landing near the Burbage Road entrance, training for local clubs started again in September.

The new tarmac surface looked good, but was not as fast as the old cement one.

The first public event on the resurfaced track was the 1945 Good Friday Meeting. With the end of the war in sight (Victory in Europe Day was only a month away on 8 May), Good Friday was once more a public holiday and there was a great feeling of optimism, making the occasion a reunion and celebration for the riders and spectators.

There was 'some fine riding' according to *Cycling* magazine. Most outstanding was Tommy Godwin, from Birmingham's Rover CC. Born in the United States but brought up in the Midlands after his parents moved back at the start of the war, Godwin was tall, muscular and possessed great stamina. He was emerging as Britain's best long-distance track cyclist: 'one of the most formidable of English path riders' according to *The Bicycle* magazine. His autobiography, *It Wasn't That Easy*, is filled with wonderful detail of this remarkable cyclist's long life in the sport. In his early career he had competed in 84 five-mile events, coming in the top three in all but one event, also winning three national titles over five and 35 miles.

(Coincidentally there was another Tommy Godwin, also from the Midlands, but born eight years earlier than the track cyclist. The 'other Tommy' was an ultra-endurance cyclist long before the term existed. In 1939 he rode a remarkable 75,065 miles, averaging over 200 miles a day, and this remains the world cycling record for miles covered in a single year.)

'I was to meet the London boys on their own "muck

heap",' the track rider wrote in his autobiography, 'and I wanted to show them that there were good "bikies" north of Watford.' After taking second place in the invitation sprint at Herne Hill, Godwin totally dominated the BSA Gold Column 5-mile points race, taking sprint after sprint to finish with a commanding lead from George Fleming, who had a number of cycling records himself. Godwin recalled:

> In 1945, my first success was my greatest, that of winning the 'five' for the BSA Gold Column at Herne Hill – the first time I had visited the Mecca of our grand game. This early success created an interest in Herne Hill for me, and I took every opportunity to compete there to get experience.

George Fleming, incidentally, was married to Billie Fleming, née Dovey, another ultra-long-distance cyclist, who had set the women's record for the greatest distance cycled in a year in 1938 at 29,603 miles. Starting from Mill Hill in London on 1 January 1938 she averaged 81 miles a day, but rode as many as 196 miles a day in summer. She was self-reliant, cycling alone and eating in cafés, and often gave public talks at the end of a long day in the saddle.

The war saw an increase in the number of women cycling competitively at Herne Hill (and indeed elsewhere), including a half-mile race for women in 1940, a women's Italian pursuit in 1941 and a half-mile handicap in 1942. But business as usual was resumed after the war as the men took centre stage again and, incredibly, it was not until 1987 that women's races were seen again on the Good Friday programme. Women's track cycling wasn't even introduced to the Olympic Games until 1988!

The official Grand Reopening Meeting was not held until 23 June 1945. It featured a France versus England competition, with victory for England secured by Tommy Godwin, Lew Pond, Ian Scott and the other great rider of this period, the sprinter Reg Harris.

Reg Harris was a phenomenon. In 1936 aged only fifteen he won the first race he ever took part in: a half-mile handicap on a grass track in his home town of Bury in Lancashire. He was selected to go to the world championships in 1939 at the Vigorelli track in Milan. But while the British team was training in the northern Italian city, war broke out and they had to return home. Harris saw action in North Africa during the war, but was invalided out in 1943 and started training again.

Harris valued the advice of his Manchester Wheelers club-mate Jack Sibbit – 'a splendid old rough diamond' – who by this stage had retired from racing and was making and selling his own bikes in Manchester. In his autobiography, *Two Wheels to the Top*, Harris recalls:

> " I often used to ride down for chats with him and I learned a tremendous amount from him. After a while he began to follow my career very closely and I used to take his advice seriously. In some ways he was the closest thing to a coach I ever had, though I never let

anyone officially be my coach – I usually preferred to do everything my own way. "

In 1944, aged 24, Harris became national track champion at two sprint distances (440 yards and 1,000 yards), but also had the stamina to win the five-mile event. He grew into the best sprinter in the world, but he could also win endurance events, as most other sprinters of his day could too. He became the superstar of his generation, eclipsing not just Godwin, but possibly any other British cyclist, ever.

Tommy Godwin and Reg Harris were the two big names often topping the same bills in this period and destined for greatness. 'I expect next to Reg, I was the biggest draw,' said Godwin, with characteristic modesty. 'I would be the gaffer in the distance races. He would have a good chance in the sprints.'

The 1945 season ended with the Meeting of Champions. After six years of inactivity, the stadium was back in business with over 8,000 fans in attendance. This was a good time to be a great cyclist. A tradesman's wage at the time was around £6–7 a week, but for leading professional racers it was quite normal to go home with the equivalent of two or three weeks' wages after a good day at a meeting.

Rather than being a luxury plaything for the rich and social elite, the bicycle during the 1920s and 1930s became a necessity for delivery boys, policemen, factory workers and housewives. In his book *On Your Bike*, James McGurn reflected on an 1895 advert for Rudge-Whitworth bicycle manufacturers which had urged customers to 'follow the fashion set by Royalty, the Aristocracy and Society'. By 1923 a Raleigh advert was asking: 'Is your life spent among whirring machinery, in adding up columns of numbers, in attending to the wants of often fractious customers? Don't you sometimes long to get away from it all? Away from the streets of serried houses …'

The bike still had the ability to thrill – as was seen by the number of chain gangs (training sessions for riders in pace lines) threading through the countryside on weekends and summer evenings. By 1939 the Cyclists' Touring Club membership was back up to 36,000, from a low point of only 8,000 in 1914.

During the Second World War road racing also finally took off. There was little traffic on the roads during the war (due to petrol rationing) and the airfields and car circuits where mass-start racing had formerly been held, were taken over by the Armed Forces, so Percy Stallard, an anti-authoritarian racing cyclist, wrote to the National Cyclists' Union requesting permission to put on a bunched road race. The NCU rejected the idea, but Stallard proceeded anyway and not only got permission from the police, but also their active help. The result was a race from Llangollen to Wolverhampton, in June 1942.

The race went ahead with 40 riders, but it plunged British cycling into a war of its own. Both the NCU and RTTC (Road Time Trials Council) suspended Stallard and all fifteen of the finishers from competing in their events in future. Stallard's response was to create the British League of Racing Cyclists (BLRC) and organise a national road race championship (which he won!). He started recruiting riders who were keen to race in massed open road 'Continental-style' races. To join the League meant being thrown out of the Union though – and often your club too. So a whole raft of new BLRC clubs were launched.

British cycling was torn in half – clubs could affiliate to BLRC or the NCU, but not both. A vitriolic seventeen-year feud between League and Union followed. BLRC was painted as the renegade group, which only served to increase its appeal to younger riders. In years to come, as rival clubs passed each other on training rides, one would shout 'Up the League', while the other would reputedly reply 'Fuck the League'.

The end of the war saw renewed enthusiasm and a further increase in the membership of cycling clubs. Track cycling in post-war Britain was to enjoy huge popularity. 'They were happy days,' remembered Godwin,

> " with refreshment tents for the public and marquees for the competitors to change in, with baths or buckets of water to wash in. Many meetings were run as works sports days on recreation grounds, others were run in conjunction with gymkhanas, dog shows and flower shows. "

Herne Hill regularly hosted works sports days such as the London Constabulary's – with bobbies riding in full uniform.

At the first peacetime Good Friday Meeting in 1946 a mile-long queue resulted in the gates being closed with a capacity crowd of 10,000 inside, and thousands turned away outside – eventually the police had to be drafted in.

Godwin shone again. Although he had good sprint ability, it wasn't his focus, showing greater speed and strength in distance races. But the Good Friday Meeting had a 550-yard invitation sprint. All the big names were there: Reg Harris, André Rivoal (the French champion), Alan Bannister, Lew Pond and John Dennis – plus Godwin. Following heats, repêchage and semis, the final saw Harris, Bannister and Godwin face each other.

Bannister led from the gun with Harris on his wheel, but Godwin was closing quickly on the back straight. With 220 yards to go Godwin managed to box in Harris on Bannister's wheel, then went for the line and held off to win. According to Bill Bailey, the retired sprint star, who was watching, as Godwin went past, Harris flicked his toe strap and claimed a mechanical fault. The gun was fired, but after some robust debate Godwin was declared the winner. He also went on to win the 5-mile points race for the second year in a row, after a dominant win in 1945, to stake his claim on the BSA Gold Column.

At a Manchester Wheelers meeting in July later that year Godwin again overtook Harris on the final bend of a 40-lap Madison and was on the home straight when he was almost stopped in his tracks by a tug on his saddle. Harris wanted to win the sprint in front of his home crowd and duly did. He was summoned to the judges, where Godwin grabbed him and pulled back his fist in front of thousands of spectators. Luckily he was restrained by Syd Cozens, a club-mate of Harris at Manchester Wheelers (who wore spectacles and a beret when he raced), but also a friend of Godwin who worked with him at BSA. Godwin suggested meeting behind the dressing rooms to settle it in private, but to no avail. The partisan judges cautioned Harris, but the result stood.

During another Madison, this time at Herne Hill, as he moved up on to Harris's shoulder, with both men at full pelt, Godwin spat out: 'You want to race? Come on then, you bastard.' He used the word in its pure sense: 'I was aware he was an illegitimate child.'

Godwin was less ruthless, but much warmer than Harris. He was a true amateur, working full-time as an electrician. He declined sponsorship from bookmakers, to his ambitious father's displeasure. Harris was a winner from the outset, who knew cycling was his route to fame and fortune – a story told by Robert Dineen in his biography of Harris, sub-titled 'The Rise and Fall of Britain's Greatest Cyclist'. Harris pushed the boundaries of amateurism and by 1945 was notionally employed by the Claud Butler cycle company, but the only work he did was ride a bike.

The financial support meant Harris could spend much of the 1945/46 winter season competing in amateur events at indoor tracks in Europe, where the style of racing was very different. In countries such as France and Belgium, sprinting was far more evolved. Match sprinting rarely involved more than three or four competitors, while prestigious events had only two – unlike the bunch sprints on flat paths in England that had changed little since Victorian times.

Harris took time to adapt to the Continental style, but appreciated its elegant nuances; the French called sprinters 'les aristocrats du cyclisme'. In Geneva in 1945 Harris was soundly beaten by a Swiss rider called Oskar Plattner, the most feted and skilful amateur cyclist of his day. According to Dineen, Harris admitted: 'I never knew what he was going to do next.' Roger St Pierre, the cycling journalist, said: 'I loved Plattner. He was a crafty little shit.'

The Good Friday Meeting traditionally marked the start of the season for many riders, although they approached it in different ways. But Godwin always tried to get in 1,500 miles training before Easter. All of his road training was done solo, but he realised in later life that he might have been a better rider had he done more group riding. In his autobiography he talked fondly of going out for group rides before the war:

> In those days when you went out, some thirty-strong in number, all were on a fixed 77-inch gear with no brakes and rode some fifty miles on a Sunday. A stop for lunch was made at Ma Copley's in Warwick, opposite the Seven Stars pub. Then there was a further

ride, going on to Aston Cantlow or Fillongley for afternoon tea, with food for 1/– a head, fruit tea 6d extra.
There was always a fast line out and a sprint to the
tea rooms. Between lunch and tea, riding through the
lanes, the big men would tell us to release our straps
to get our feet out quickly. Then a session of wheel
rubbing in the bunch, senior riders leaning on to us
trying to ditch us, cutting across front wheels, all to
teach us good bike handling. 🙶

In 1947 the promoter Jim Wallace contracted sixteen top
Continental professionals to join the Good Friday Meeting,
in an attempt to bring back its international flavour. A handsome man with dark hair slicked back, arched eyebrows and
a wide smile topped off with a pencil moustache, he preferred to select riders on merit, so there were no handicap
races, instead including six foreign amateurs (three of whom
were national champions), Reg Harris, Tommy Godwin and
others.

A large gate of 11,000 spectators were ironically disap-
pointed by the professionals (many of whom, with unfortunate
timing, had only just finished a six-day race in Belgium late
the previous night), but the amateurs saved the day. Harris
was facing two top riders: Ray Pauwels of Belgium and Cor
Bijster, who had beaten Harris in the quarter-finals of the
world championship in Zurich the previous year. Harris won
the Good Friday Sprint, but Pauwels won the special three-up
sprint between the top men. The final amateur ride of the day

was the 5-mile points race for the BSA Gold Column. All the top amateurs were riding: Godwin won.

Meanwhile a run of six national track titles saw Harris selected for the 1947 world amateur sprint championships, which he won with ease. He was ready to prove his dominance at professional level, but the London Olympics were just around the corner and he became the red-hot favourite to win gold in the three sprint disciplines.

# 6

## Toad-in-the-hole and tight shorts

Despite the desperate shortage of resources and materials across Europe following the war, the International Olympic Committee decided that the next Olympic Games would be held in 1948 in London. The British public mostly disapproved of the government's decision to host the competition, which came to be known as the 'Austerity Games'. Staging an event that would cost £750,000 seemed irresponsible when people were still surviving on food and energy rations, 2 million were unemployed and there was a housing shortage. 'The average range of British enthusiasms for the Games stretches from lukewarm to dislike,' complained the *Evening Standard* in 1947. 'It is not too late for invitations to be politely withdrawn.'

But support gradually grew and ultimately a record 59 nations were represented by 4,104 athletes (3,714 men and 390 women) in nineteen disciplines over 136 different events between 29 July and 14 August 1948.

The cycling competition consisted of two road cycling events and four track cycling events: sprint, tandem sprint, team pursuit and kilometre time trial. The road race events were held in Windsor Great Park and the track cycling events were held at Herne Hill – which remains the only venue from those Games still in use today.

Britain had won medals in track cycling at every Olympics since London 1908 when they won five golds (except for 1912 in Stockholm, which was the only Games not to include track cycling). But there had been no individual gold wins since 1908, just one for the tandem in 1920 and a silver and bronze from each of the following three Games, until 1936 when they won a solitary bronze. Nonetheless, the discipline was a high hope for medals in 1948 and the National Cyclists' Union proclaimed: 'Not one Olympic title must leave this country!'

The Olympics were still restricted to amateur riders in 1948 (they weren't opened to professionals until 1996 in Atlanta), but Reg Harris, by this stage, was keen to turn professional. Sprinters were paid lucrative appearance fees across Europe throughout the year, and enjoyed sponsorship deals. The best time to graduate was after winning the world amateur title in 1947, but 1948 would be Harris's last opportunity to appear in the Olympics, where he could realistically hope to win three events: the sprint, the kilometre time trial and the tandem sprint.

Being selected as an Olympic venue provided funds for a complete makeover at Herne Hill. The track was relaid yet again, this time in bitumen. Plans were made for extensive refurbishments, a new side stand, turnstiles, car and cycle parks, refreshments rooms, toilets and press facilities. The standing areas around the outside of the track were enlarged to accommodate 15,000.

Great plans were laid for the 1948 Good Friday Meeting as a showcase for the first-class riders and facilities that the world would be enjoying in August. It was an outstanding success. The highlight was the pitting of current world champion Reg Harris against likely contenders for Olympic honours: an event for all the national amateur sprint champions that would herald a Champion of Champions.

Promoter Jim Wallace negotiated sponsorship with the *News of the World* for the Champion of Champions race, and they were joined by a number of other sponsors for other races. Several riders had recently turned professional, leaving Axel Schandorff of Denmark and Mario Ghella of Italy as Harris's main competitors. Wallace also introduced a new event that year, inviting comparatively young or unknown riders to compete in the White Hope Sprint in the desire that he could unearth future stars. It went on to provide the launch pad for a great many champions through the years.

But disaster struck: on his way to London from Manchester, Harris's sports car crashed. He fractured two vertebrae, his legs were paralysed and the doctors swore he'd never walk again, let alone ride a bike. The race was eventually won by an outsider, eighteen-year-old Jan Hijselendoorn from Holland.

His training had been curtailed, but remarkably Harris

recovered quickly enough to start riding again in a few weeks and resumed his training – leading some of his detractors to speculate that the injury was exaggerated. But then he crashed on Fallowfield track on 10 July – just weeks before the Games. It was far from ideal preparation.

Athletes began arriving for the Games in July. No new venues were built, and the athletes were housed in existing accommodation instead of an Olympic Village, as was the case in the 1936 Games and later in 1952. Teams were billeted all over London in schools, hostels and private houses, with transport arranged to the stadiums. Men were predominantly put up in RAF digs in Uxbridge and Richmond, while the women stayed in accommodation around the city centre. Rationing was still in force and packages were sent from all over the world to help the Olympic cause.

'About six weeks before the Olympics, our rations were increased,' remembered Robert Maitland, a member of the British road cycling team quoted in Janie Hampton's book about the 1948 Games:

> 66 We had six ounces of meat a day, one pound of pota-
> toes, half an ounce of bacon, two ounces of sugar,
> one of preserves, one of cheese, one third of tea, one
> tenth of dried eggs, two pints of milk, one pound of
> bread, and once a week, half a pound of sweets or
> chocolates. 99

The New Zealand team travelled furthest to the Olympics.

Before setting out on the five-week journey by boat via the Panama Canal, each athlete had signed an Olympic bond promising they would 'win without swank and lose without grousing'. They also promised not to become professionals for at least two years after the Games and to share as much learning about their sport upon their return as possible. It was a bad Atlantic crossing, although the cyclist Nick Carter had rollers built on deck. 'That gave me some exercise. I had ropes mounted for stability in case the boat lurched. But it was hard to ride with the side to side motion of the boat. I couldn't ride at all if the roll was too great.'

Through the summer of 1948 enthusiasm for the Olympics slowly grew, as the best cyclists in the country competed for a place in the squad. Managed by Bill Bailey, the former sprint champion, the track team spent the fortnight before the Games at Herne Hill on a training camp, although in reality Bailey was conducting last-minute trials to see who would make the final team.

The British track cycling team were spared the daily commute from west London to Herne Hill by Bill Mills, editor of *The Bicycle*, who put them up in his large house on Half Moon Lane in Herne Hill. 'We slept in the loft, which was once the servants' quarters, on camp beds,' remembers Jim Love, a pursuit rider who was reserve on the Olympic team. He was a smooth, fast rider who should probably have been on the pursuit team, but the fact that he was only nineteen (much younger than anyone else) and of small build – in fact known as 'the boy' – perhaps explains why he never got to ride.

'We just had to go down the garden, open the back gate and we're in the track,' he says. Many of the large houses still had gates leading into the stadium grounds, to provide access to allotments started during the war. Godwin's mother, Dora, provided the meals – spam fritters for breakfast, then toad-in-the-hole and rice pudding for tea. There was much camaraderie in the group that stayed there, but Harris of course had booked into his favourite hotel in St John's Wood instead.

Harris also had to undergo a trial because he had been picked for the individual sprint and tandem sprint on condition that he proved his fitness. He had not been selected for the kilometre time trial, because it was scheduled immediately after the tandem sprint – leaving Godwin to fill the place. Harris did not arrive at Herne Hill until a week into preparations. He did two sprint trials and his performance was perfect. He promptly left the track and said that he was returning to Manchester. Bailey left a message at the hotel demanding that he stay in London with the team. 'I've proven my fitness,' Harris said. 'I'm going home for the week, that will be the best way for me to prepare.' He made countless excuses but the truth, he later admitted, was that he was struggling to regain fitness and could only run a few sprints before a sharp decline. According to Robert Dineen's research into the episode, Harris didn't want his opponents to see that weakness:

> " It seems to me poor strategy to be carrying out my training routine on a track where the terraces were

lined with all the other riders and officials from the competing nations. That's a great thing if you're going to destroy everybody in sight and demoralise the entire entry. But I wasn't really that good.  "

When he arrived home he received another warning phone call, which he ignored, carrying on his training in Manchester. The issue escalated: Adrian Chamberlain, the committee chairman, gave him until 6pm to return to London – again Harris dug in his heels. As Britain's only world champion in an Olympic event, he knew he was Britain's best bet for a medal.

Needless to say he stayed in Manchester and by the next day it was headline news in the tabloids, surpassing interest in live events. The *Daily Mirror* quoted Harris: 'Unless I can train with my own lads here on the ground I've used for 16 years, I can't get Olympic form. If the worst comes, I'll sit in the stand.'

The NCU threat to remove him from the team was widely known, but many people saw it as an unnecessarily bureaucratic stance. Even Christopher Wood, the team doctor, had argued that Harris would benefit more from a week at home. Harris, predictably, remained unrepentant. 'It's ridiculous to say my actions upset the rest of the team,' he told the press. 'I'm not a member of a team. I'm an individual sprinter and I can't see that any grown man should be upset by what I've done.'

The final compromise was a suggestion that Harris ride a

race-off with Alan Bannister for the Olympic sprint selection. Although the race was supposed be secret, there were several hundred spectators including the press waiting for him at Herne Hill on the appointed evening. Harris and Bannister were opposites in most respects, not just physically (Bannister was short and slight) but also temperamentally. Bannister was modest to a fault, a trait which the arrogant Harris exploited ruthlessly. He phoned before the race expressing his contempt and the inconvenience of having to prove his superiority. 'If I've got to come down and demonstrate my ability to beat you, it will do no good to either of us.'

When Harris arrived at Herne Hill, the mind games continued. He unveiled his new Raleigh earlier than expected (it was planned that he should do so at the Games), and played cat and mouse with Bannister in such a vicious manner that it seemed more designed to shred Bannister's nerves than to simply win a race. But Harris did win, attacking once he was convinced Bannister had been unnerved. The second heat followed the same format, and that was it. Bannister was fitter and faster than Harris at the time according to most accounts, but Harris won 'by sheer personality' according to Alan Geldard, a member of the pursuit team.

The Olympic track cycling started at the end of the first week of the Games on Saturday 7 August, with the sprint and team pursuits up to quarter-finals. On Monday 9 August the sprint and team pursuits were continued up to and including

the finals, plus the tandem prelims and repêchage. Then
Wednesday 11 August saw the tandem sprint up to and including the finals and the kilometre time trial.

Keen club men volunteered to be whips, but had to buy
their own uniforms for the privilege. The blazer, trousers and
tie ensemble cost more than a grandstand seat! Herne Hill
itself was in good order. By this time an additional temporary
stand made of planks and scaffolding with seating for 200–300
more had appeared along the back straight. Flags from each
participating nation were hoisted around the perimeter of
the track. And despite a ban on advertising elsewhere in the
Olympics, 'DUNLOP' was still visible in eight-foot-high let-
ters on the banking.

There was also a photo-finish camera mounted on a
tower which overlooked the finish line, and 'automatic
timing'. Basically the starter's pistol was connected to an
electro-mechanical device, which started two watches when
the gun was fired. The rider broke a thread as he crossed
the finish line which released a spring-controlled lever and
automatically stopped the watches. Riders could be timed to
tenths of a second.

On Saturday 7 August rain was falling steadily. This kept
many people in the café – which over the four days reputedly
served 13,400 cups of tea, 16,150 sandwiches and buns, and
12,200 ice creams.

For the first time the match sprint was conducted as the
best of three races. Harris progressed easily through the preliminary rounds against the Indian cyclist Ruston Mullafiroze

and the Chilean Mario Masanés. Both were dispatched with Harris displaying consummate tactical superiority.

The other side of the draw featured the nineteen-year-old Italian student Mario Ghella, who also needed only two races to dispatch his opponents. In both cases he used the same simple tactic: launch an improbably devastating sprint with 300 metres to go, leaving his opponents for dead.

In the last sixteen of the sprint event, L. Rocca of Uruguay and Jan Hijselendoorn of Holland both crashed yards from the finish. Hijselendoorn tried to block as Rocca overtook on the inside. The Dutchman fell first, but then the Uruguayan also fell, sliding along the track to cross the line first! Rocca was disqualified for overtaking on the inside, but the decision was challenged by the Uruguayan team and a rerun scheduled for the next day.

Alan Geldard, Tommy Godwin, David Ricketts and Wilf Waters represented Great Britain in the 4,000-metre team pursuit. Geldard, a 21-year-old commercial artist from Oldham, had never even ridden in a team pursuit before. Janie Hampton reported his description of the experience:

> We were still being trialled in the last fortnight … The team everyone feared was Italy but they had one super rider and the others couldn't keep up. You need a blend of four equal riders. If we had got our act together we might have won the gold, but our officials didn't know what the team pursuit was, so we were still learning as we competed.

Geldard continued:

     We owned our own bikes. They were good-quality steel tubing, made especially for us with drop handles and no gears, brakes or mudguards. Punctures were rare because the tyres were made of thick rubber with no inner tube. The frame cost two weeks' wages. The only contribution we got was Dunlop lent us tyres and then after the Games they were taken back. If Dunlop had used our names in their advertisements it would have compromised our amateur status. We didn't get any sponsorship or expenses at all. We had no coaching whatsoever. You just worked at it hard and if you were any good you continued up the ladder to selection.

Nonetheless Great Britain were a fine team, beating Denmark in the quarter-final and then facing France in the semi-final. 'We led early on, in a very fast start to the race,' wrote Godwin in his autobiography:

     and until about half-way were up by about three lengths. Then, suddenly in one lap, they pulled us back and took a two-length lead. I responded by taking a hard, fast turn to close the deficit. As I swung up the banking Wilf Waters kicked through instead of just maintaining the increased speed. I came down to drop on the back and there was a gap I could not close, try as I may. Our remaining three went on, losing distance all the time. I was distraught. I was proud of my strength, my ability and consideration for other team members. I felt I was in disgrace, and not justifiably, a team mate had worked me over. **"**

✹

On the second day of track racing, a capacity crowd packed the track to see the sprint and team pursuit finals. By the end of the first week, Britain was still without a gold in any discipline and by the time Harris arrived at Herne Hill on Monday of the second week, there was an increasing desperation for a champion to emerge from the home nation's team. As the current world champion, hopes were high for the gold medal despite the fact the Harris had not had a good year.

The weather was fine – more so than the construction company had envisaged: the tarmac began to soften in places as the temperature hit 80 degrees. Dineen spoke to Brian Annable, who went on to race in the 1952 Helsinki Olympics himself and earned an OBE in 2013 for lifelong services to British cycling as a promoter and coach; Annable was volunteering at the track that day. He had spent two days cycling to London from Leicester, sleeping with friends in a barn on the way. 'I was on the railway banking, standing in the trees,' he said of the occasion. 'There were thousands of us, umpteen deep, all standing. The atmosphere was unbelievable.'

In the first sprint semi-final Ghella showed yet more blistering pace to beat the Dane Axel Schandorff. Harris thrashed the Australian Charlie Bazzano, leaving the final match that most fans wanted.

Harris was first on to the track, looking confident and relaxed with Brylcreemed dark hair and his parting just off-centre as he waved to the crowd. He wore NCU regulation-issue black shorts and his heavy woollen world champion's rainbow jersey – a far cry from the skin-suits his countrymen would wear 60 years later in Beijing, and entirely inappropriate for racing in 80-degree heat.

After a ten-minute wait Ghella eventually came out in the most bizarre and suspicious manner. With thick dark hair and brown lifeless eyes, wearing the blue Italian jersey, he was carried from the changing room beneath the stands by two assistants, his arms draped over their shoulders and his legs hanging limp. A third helper wheeled his bike. 'He was doped to the eyeballs,' said Alan Geldard. 'They didn't want it pumping through his system until he needed it.'

There followed a battle to out-psyche each other. First the Italians went through an elaborate examination of the bike, double-checking for faults. Harris meanwhile joked with the crowd, and then once Ghella was ready he in turn pretended there were problems with his bicycle.

In the first race, Ghella stuck to his tactic of jumping with 300 metres to go. Although Harris was expecting this, he was clearly shocked at the sheer ferocity of Ghella's kick. The moment's hesitation left him five lengths behind on the final bend and with 50 metres to go, to the incredulity of the crowd, he sat up on the home straight in front of the grandstand.

In the next race Ghella was more cautious at the start, slowing almost to a standstill, hoping that Harris would take the lead, but Harris was having none of it and when Ghella jumped on the bend as usual, he was ready. Harris stayed in his slipstream, launching attack after attack. There was a mixture of silent disbelief and raucous encouragement from the partisan crowd as he passed them, but without effect. He trailed at the finish line by two lengths.

In two straight rides Ghella became the new Olympic champion and Harris took silver: a bitter blow to British pride and Harris's ego. Ghella was showered with kisses and held aloft, while Harris fled to the changing room to tend his wounded pride. 'I am certain no other English rider could have done better,' he told the press, ungraciously defending himself, blaming his injuries, lack of racing and thwarted training in the build-up. He also promised to beat Ghella in the upcoming world championships in Amsterdam.

'It appears and was alleged that Ghella did not win unaided,' recalled Godwin. 'For each ride he was physically carried to his bike on the start line by two beefy Italians. When he finished each ride he was carried from the track to a seat in the Italian camp.' Although he conceded: 'A very fast, smooth riding Italian sprinter is a pleasure to witness. Ghella's times through the series were outstanding.'

Ghella actually went on to win the world amateur championship later in August, beating Harris into third place behind Schandorff, but then disappeared from the scene, whereas Harris turned professional and had a distinguished career for another ten years, including four world professional championship wins.

The other final on day two was the 4,000-metre team pursuit. Sixteen teams had been reduced to the semi-finals of Italy v. Uruguay and France v. Great Britain. The two best pursuit teams in the world at the time were France and Italy. France had won the gold medal in 1936, while Italy had won four consecutive Olympics titles from 1920 to 1932. A year before the Olympics, France had defeated the British team by over two seconds at Herne Hill. In the first semi-final France defeated Britain again, by just under five seconds; the second semi was no closer, with Italy winning by almost six seconds.

In the minor final for bronze the Englishmen seemed tired according to *Cycling* magazine, until:

> " Godwin put in a steaming half-lap, then Waters another flier, and the margin was reduced. The 'home' riders were now riding like demons, a remarkable recovery, and in lap six, a one-second lead, then a gain of three seconds, when the opposition cracked, lap eight another 2.5 seconds. The bell and the four Englishmen went on to finish in grand formation, winning by half the length of the straight in 4.55.8, the second fastest of the series, France's time in the final was 4.57.8. "

In the final, the Italian team cracked in the face of a consummate performance from the French team; *Cycling* described the race as a farce. Although the Italians got off quickly, and were still leading by four lengths after seven laps, France overturned their advantage and were leading convincingly into the bell lap, when Arnaldo Benfenati responded with a tremendous kick.

> " That one sudden effort was the Italians' downfall. They opened out like a concertina. The crowd shouted but to no avail. Benfenati was miles in front, his team mates, shattered, sat up. In fact, one rider nearly stopped and one of their officials ran across, took hold of the saddle and bars, and proceeded to push the rider around the track to the finish line, a time of 5.36.6. "

As the time in the team pursuit is taken when the third rider crosses the line, France won by almost 40 seconds.

❋

The 1,000-metre time trial was held on the third and final day of track racing. Before the race the Belgian coach Louis Gerlash gave Godwin a massage and offered him 'something to help win the gold'. Godwin was furious. Amphetamines were available and there were no blood tests at the Games. Doping became widespread after the war as military drugs flooded the market and by the early 1950s professional riders were openly consuming drugs in full view of spectators and competitors.

Jacques Dupont of France went on to win the time trial with 1 minute 13.5 seconds; one second ahead of Pierre Nihant of Belgium, with Godwin winning his second bronze medal of the Games only half a second behind.

The 2,000-metre tandem race was also on the last day, and the final itself was widely considered to be the most exciting track race of the Games. Hopes for the tandem sprint were pinned on the reigning world sprint champion Reg Harris, riding with Alan Bannister, the man he had humiliated in the sprint trial only days earlier. They were the 1947 British champions, but Harris had to regain his self-confidence quickly having lost the sprint final in such convincing manner. Tandem partners are usually of similar stature to ensure balance and harmony. On paper Bannister and Harris were far from harmonious, physically or personally, but as the two fastest men in their club they were paired together and it worked. Bannister was light and fast, so rode 'stoker', while the explosive and decisive Harris led from the front.

Unsurprisingly, they barely spoke as they rode through the early rounds of the event. They faced the French favourites, Gaston Dron and René Faye in the semi-finals, which were conducted as a single race. The British pair were preparing to attack when their front tyre punctured – a serious prospect on a tandem given the weight, speed and awkwardness. But they managed to keep the bike upright as it swerved around the track. When the race was rerun, they defeated the French team by a length. In the other semi-final Italy easily defeated Switzerland, winning by six lengths.

Before the final, the best of three races against the Italian pair of Renato Perona and Ferdinando Terruzzi, Harris was confident, declaring: 'We will win.' Terruzzi was sprint champion of Lombardy and a canny tactician. He was already 34 years old but would continue competing in professional six-day races until he was 50, winning 21 six-days with various partners. But he met his match in Harris, who in the first race drifted slightly towards the Italian pair. Not enough to attract disapproval from the judges, but enough to check their confidence moments before the British pair attacked and went on to win.

In the second race Terruzzi took advantage of a momentary lapse of concentration from Harris to attack and win, securing level pegging. As dusk settled the prospect of delaying the final race until the following day was discussed, but amid vociferous jeers and protest from the crowd once they realised what was being considered – and the realisation that there was no funding for a further day's racing anyway – it was finally settled. There were no floodlights, so cars were brought in to shine their headlights on the track. The British white singlets were visible, but Terruzzi and Perona were almost invisible in their navy blue.

The race lived up to the expectation of the crowd, with the lead swapping repeatedly between the two pairs. The bikes were neck and neck until the bell, when Harris and Bannister jumped and went flat out into the back straight. At the 220-metre mark they had a lead of 1½ lengths as they disappeared into the dusky gloom of the final bend. As the

The start of a race for safety bikes, 1895.
Press Association

The start of a race in the early 1900s with Leon Meredith in white (second left).
Jim Love Archive

Harry Wyld during a tandem-paced record attempt in the 1920s.
Jim Love Archive

J.W. Holdsworth in a 24-hour tandem-paced record attempt
(after puncture repair), 1927.
Jim Love Archive

Frank Southall and Harry Wyld competing in a motor-paced event, March 1929.
Mary Evans/Imagno

The 30-mile race at the annual Metropolitan Police sports day, 1929.
Mary Evans/Imagno

Lyons Tea Shop waitresses – known as 'nippies' – race in 1930.
Mary Evans/Imagno

Old-timers' penny-farthing race, 1933.
Mary Evans/Imagno

Dennis Horn at the 21st annual Meeting of Champions, 1933.
Mary Evans/Imagno

Toni Merkens and Wilf Higgins fight it out ahead of Dennis Horn in the sprint
omnium on Good Friday 1935.
Jim Love Archive

The start of an ordinary/penny-farthing race, 1930s.

A capacity crowd at the Good Friday Meeting in 1946.
Jim Love Archive

Reg Harris (far left), Cor Byster (centre) and Ray Pauwels, Good Friday 1947.
Jim Love Archive

Mario Ghella (left) and Henri Sensever in
the international sprint at Good Friday 1948.
Jim Love Archive

Reg Harris (nearest rider) heading for victory against Mario Masanés of Chile in the
preliminary round of the sprint at the 1948 Olympics.
Jim Love Archive

(RIGHT) Start of the sprint semi-final, where Reg Harris beat Charlie Bazzano of Australia.
Jim Love Archive

(BELOW) Reg Harris leads Mario Ghella on the back straight in front of the temporary stand, Olympic sprint final, 1948.
Jim Love Archive

Great Britain catching the Canadians in the first round of the team pursuit, 1948.
Jim Love Archive

The GB team at the start of the team pursuit minor final against Uruguay:
Tommy Godwin, Wilf Waters, Dave Ricketts and Alan Geldard, 1948.
Jim Love Archive

The Great Britain pursuit team wins bronze.
From left to right: Alan Geldard, Tommy Godwin, Dave Ricketts and Wilf Waters.
Jim Love Archive

Wilf Waters (outside lane), Dave Ricketts (inside lane) and others line up before
being introduced to the crowd at the start of the Dunlop meeting, 1950.
Jim Love Archive

Enzo Sacchi, being paced by a Lambretta scooter, 1958.
Mortons Archive

Fausto Coppi in the final race of the 1959 meeting.
Jim Love

The Devil race at the second 'Coppi meeting'.
From left to right: Guido Messina, André Darrigarde, John Geddes,
Rik van Steenbergen, Fred de Bruyne, Fausto Coppi and Brian Robinson.
Jim Love

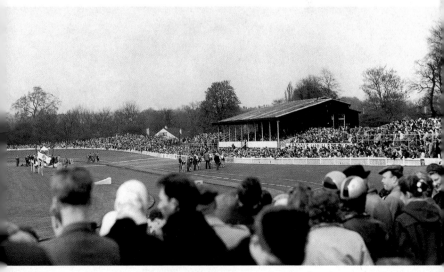

Race day in 1960.
Jim Love Archive

(ABOVE) Tom Simpson and
Barry Hoban, Good Friday
1963.
Keith Waldegrave

Graeme Obree at Good
Friday 1994, wearing
his world champion's
rainbow jersey.
Phil O'Connor

Bradley Wiggins winning the 10-minute pursuit, Good Friday 2003.
Jim Love

Two sixteen-year-olds, Fred Wright and Ethan Hayter, battle it out at senior track league 2015 – both are now in the Olympic development programme.
Phil Wright

Young girl at Derny Fest 2015.
Phil Wright

The sun sets on the old grandstand at a track league meeting, 2015.
Phil Wright

Italians made a last supreme effort the crowd went wild in hope of a gold medal on the final day of track cycling. The riders were almost invisible to most of the spectators on the grandstand, who fell quiet, until the pairs emerged shoulder to shoulder thundering down the home straight and were neck and neck at the line.

Although the partisan crowd was clear that the British tandem had crossed the line first, in reality it was almost impossible to split the pairs. The photo-finish facility had been turned off due to the risk of blinding the riders in the twilight, and it was left to the international panel of judges to make the call. After a while the officials decided in favour of the Italians – and Britain had failed to win gold yet again. The crowd left in despair as darkness fell.

The final tally was four medals in track cycling: silver in the sprint and tandem, bronze in the time trial and team pursuit. There may have been no gold medals, but every team member was a medal winner.

A celebratory dinner in London a week later, however, descended into a slanging match once Lew Pond, a reserve on the track team, criticised the officials' inadequate preparation. Once the floodgates were open many riders spoke out in support, venting their frustration at the amateurism of 'the blazer brigade' at the National Cyclists' Union.

'Nobody ever coached us,' says Jim Love. 'They never even said who had done a fast lap or a slow lap.' They only had a fortnight's training; Tommy Godwin reckoned if they'd had a month, they'd have won the team pursuit gold. But

Love laughs about it now: the equipment was so poor that one competitor (who remains nameless to spare any blushes) was unable to race because his borrowed shorts were too tight!

'Being at Herne Hill was the thrill of a lifetime. I was given permission to take three weeks off for the Olympics,' remembered Geldard wistfully in Janie Hampton's account of the Austerity Olympics, 'but when I went back with my medal, I was sacked for taking time off. There was no company pride in having a medal winner; I was just inconvenient.'

# 7

# The glamour boys

After the Olympic medal ceremony Tommy Godwin walked home to the house in Herne Hill where the team was staying: 'I had a cup of Horlicks and then went to bed.' Reg Harris, meanwhile, wasted no time putting the Games behind him: he turned professional in September 1948 for Raleigh, and went on to take the professional world by storm. On his return to Herne Hill in 1949, Harris thrashed Mario Ghella by ten lengths in their first meeting since the world amateur championships – setting the tone for their comparative performance as professionals.

Harris ruled the roost from 1949 until 1954, winning four world sprint titles. With panache, huge legs and swagger, he became a household name throughout the 1950s, as famous in his day as 'brand Beckham'. He was voted Sportsman of the Year by the Sports Journalists' Association and BBC Sports Personality of the Year twice. The advertising slogan 'Reg rides a Raleigh' was universal. He was made a hero of *Eagle* and *Boy's Own Paper* and policemen stopped errant kids on bikes, saying: 'Who do you think you are, Reg Harris?' He was earning well over £12,000 a year, when the average wage was only £500.

In the post-war years, there were only really six sports that enjoyed any real degree of professional status: boxing, cricket, golf, horse racing, football – and cycling. 'When I started there were two ways into the sport of cycling,' said Brian Annable, the 1952 Olympic rider interviewed by Richard Moore for his history of Britain's track cycling revolution, *Heroes, Villains & Velodromes*:

> " On the road you had the inspiration of the Tour de France, the mountains and all the rest of it. But in Britain at that time you couldn't road race – massed start racing on the road was banned. You could time trial or ride on the track, and track racing was huge. Heavyweight boxers and sprint cyclists were superstars in those days. "

The 1949 Good Friday Meeting was a roll-call of world and Olympic champions with Harris making his first professional appearance against his most enduring rival, the reigning world sprint champion Arie van Vliet. The Dutchman won four world championship gold medals in his career, set several world records, and at the 1936 Olympics in Berlin won a gold medal in the kilometre time trial and a silver medal in the individual sprint. Their rivalry became the final heyday of professional sprinting.

Also racing was Sid Patterson, the popular Australian rider who had represented Australia at the 1948 Olympics and would go on to win world titles as an amateur and professional. He arrived 24 hours before the meeting, looking overweight and out of condition after several weeks on the boat. But he won several races including the BSA Gold Column.

Harris, meanwhile, would go on to win the world professional sprint title in Copenhagen in August 1949 – the first British rider ever to do so. It was to be the start of a hugely successful professional career: he would go on to win in Liège the next year, then Milan the year after, to make it three in a row. He would then take the title a further time in 1954 in Cologne, before retiring from professional racing in 1957.

Harris and van Vliet met in the semi-final in Copenhagen rather than the final as most of the spectators would have expected and wished for. Although Harris was the newcomer, it was van Vliet who was the most riled at facing his strongest competitor in the semi-final rather than the final. He remonstrated long and hard with the officials, but to no avail. Harris took strength from the apparent discomfort of the usually calm 'professor' (who had shown steely calm when refusing to shake Hitler's hand at the 1936 Olympics), and when the time eventually came to race it was Harris who winked insouciantly at the press box.

However, in the first of three heats, van Vliet won by three lengths after a lapse of concentration from Harris. The Englishman's tactics were vastly improved in the second heat, however: he controlled the race from the front and launched a devastating attack at the perfect moment. In the third and final race, Harris again appeared to have a lapse in concentration: when he glanced into the crowd, van Vliet attacked. But this time, despite a decent gap, Harris was able to launch his trademark double-jump to a gasp from the crowd and from van Vliet himself. Harris won by three lengths.

The double-jump essentially involves producing an extra explosion of acceleration: a second jump, just when your opponent assumes you are travelling at top speed. Harris could feign exhaustion, creating a false sense of security in his competitor, then destroy their spirit with a further devastating kick. 'The Englishman has no equal for producing two or three bursts in one sprint,' *L'Equipe* said. 'It appears that he is passed or being held and then suddenly he flashes past his rivals.'

The other semi-final was between Jan Derksen, another Dutch cyclist who had been world professional track sprint champion in 1946 (and would win again in 1957), and Louis Gérardin. Derksen was the winner, but he was subsequently annihilated by Harris in the final in two straight races, the second of which produced a new record. It was a fitting way for Harris to become the first ever rider to win the professional title in his debut season.

Van Vliet came from a wealthier background than Harris and hadn't ridden a bike until his brother persuaded him to, but a year later had become kilometre champion at the 1936 Olympics in Berlin. They both made a good living out of their rivalry, with Harris identifying van Vliet's weakness as 'never having been out in a cape and sou'wester and ridden in the rain for eight hours'.

Whereas nowadays riders would probably aim to peak at the world championships and then take a well-earned break from racing, in those days that was the last thing on their minds. High-profile wins were followed by a small window of opportunity to earn a fortune in so-called 'revenge races' against the other semi-finalists. As world champion Harris could command much higher appearance fees, and the racing was easy as these exhibition matches were generally fixed – allowing the elite riders to win in front of their appreciative home crowds.

In Aarhus and Amsterdam spectators cheered van Vliet's revenge for the world championships as he swept Harris to the side; in Paris Gérardin won; and back on Harris's home soil in Fallowfield, Manchester a week later the local man triumphed again. But in the spirit of showmanship the races were as exciting as possible and in the spirit of comradeship no riders were humiliated. At Herne Hill, van Vliet won the first race by half a wheel. Harris won the second by inches. In the third race, Harris trailed van Vliet until the very last moment before launching an attack and shot through to win by a bike length.

Seasoned track riders could see what was happening, but to the crowd it was just top-notch racing and they loved it. 'You had to be really on the button to realise it,' says Jim Love. 'It was very convincing. These guys were no fools. They needed the appearance money.' There's much speculation about how many races were fixed on the professional circuit – hence its nickname 'the circus' – and certainly many of them were.

After a two-year gap where the world title was won by Oscar Plattner and van Vliet again, Harris went on to win his fourth world sprint title in Cologne in 1954. In those days there were separate titles for amateurs and professionals. As Harris won his final professional crown, Britain also provided the amateur winner – Cyril Peacock, a south London glass-blower, who beat John Tressider of Australia and Roger Gaignard of France.

An outstanding sprinter with brushed-back, dark brown hair and a prominent widow's peak, in 1952 Peacock had been the first Englishman to win the £1,000 International Champion of Champions sprint at the Good Friday Meeting. Sponsored by the *News of the World* it was the most valuable trophy in international cycle racing at the time. He also beat the French champion André Beyney in France, and in July won the British sprint championship, again at Herne Hill. That brought selection for Britain in the 1952 Olympic Games in Helsinki, where he just missed out on a bronze behind Enzo Sacchi of Italy, Lionel Cox of Australia and Werner Putzenheim of Germany. He won the national championship again in 1953 and 1954, and the Champion of Champions sprint again in 1953.

So Britain ruled the world of sprint cycling in 1954 – considered by many to be the blue riband of track cycling. But

Harris and Peacock were to be the last British winners before Chris Hoy in 2008.

While the 'Reg Harris phenomenon' only affected track cycling's popularity when he actually appeared, there was still a thriving race scene at Herne Hill. Professionals were coaxed to the track for a regular season of top-quality Saturday meetings, including world champions such as Harris, van Vliet, Patterson, Plattner, Derksen and Arnold, top Continental six-day riders and leading national track cyclists. Top amateurs supported the races – but by invitation only. As a result the quality and competitiveness of the regular Monday and Wednesday night race leagues benefitted, as leading riders fought for selection to face the professionals on the weekend. Big meetings attracted big crowds as they always had, but top hats and bowlers, or straw boaters and fedoras, had been replaced by bare heads and greased hair with the odd flat cap; woollen suits had been replaced by shirtsleeves – or even short sleeves.

At the world championships in Amsterdam in 1956, at a time when there were no rules about how long riders could remain stationary in a track stand at the start of a sprint as they sought to force their competitors to take the first move, Harris and Plattner defied slow handclaps to stay in position for 31 minutes! Once the track stand world record was broken they were moved back to the line to start again – it was obvious neither would crack.

A meeting in September 1949 promoted by Catford CC marked the first appearance of Harris at Herne Hill since winning the professional world sprint championship. He easily beat New Zealander Andrew Priestly in the sprints.

There was also a series of motor-paced races with Harry Grant and Wally Summers of England matched against Guy Bethery and Georges Sérès of France, four-up behind the big Triumph motorbikes racing at 45mph. Bethery emerged the overall winner of motor-paced events. The meeting also boasted an appearance by Margaret Sutcliffe, 'the red-haired lady from Paris' (according to the publicity), who set new ladies' motor-paced records from 1 to 10 miles.

Tommy Godwin, meanwhile, was by no means resting on his laurels after the Olympics. He was in fine form in the tandem-paced race, which provided one of the biggest thrills of the afternoon against a high-quality international field:

> The audacity of my ride was when my pacing tandem was too slow. I jumped in behind another rider, following his tandem for one lap until a faster team came on and in the final lap, although leading, I actually jumped past my own pacing tandem in the last 220 yards.

But Godwin went about his career in a much more modest way than Harris. 'Reg was possibly the most hated and disliked member of the track racing fraternity,' he said, 'and yet immensely popular with the public and the media.' He was known as 'Sir Reg' on account of his incongruous cut-glass accent and debonair dress style, although he was anything but a gentleman: utterly ruthless in pursuit of victory and not above skulduggery and dubious tactics.

Godwin claimed Harris would go to unacceptable lengths to win (although everybody broke the rules to some degree then). He describes a day at the popular Whit Tuesday meeting at The Butts in Coventry. He saw Harris, Sensever, Babinet and Lanners (three French riders) drawing straws to see who should be the winner of the 5-mile Dunlop Cup, of which Godwin was the holder. Three riders would help one to win. But Sensever punctured and crashed, Harris swung up on to the concrete wall, snapping his right pedal off, then Lanners and Babinet were involved in a spill with Lew Pond. Godwin described going 'merrily on my way to win'. But he wasn't happy:

> " I was becoming somewhat disenchanted with the manner in which the sport was being manipulated. Some judges' decisions were overlooking the rules, there were arranged rides, with riders being approached to gang up on one rider. I had always ridden with a strong mind, a superb physical condition and a will to win. But I was finding out how some people resorted to fixing races to suit individuals or to suppress ability. "

Godwin hated the fact that Harris sold his trophies, as well as his prizes. To Godwin this was to disrespect the event. Harris preferred material wealth as a measure of success. Godwin also disliked his attitude towards women. Whereas Godwin had been married since he was 24 and took his family duties very seriously, Harris married three times and was drawn to pretty women. Godwin recalled in his autobiography how his own father dragged him from the girls who used to gather after events:

> We'd come out of the dressing room and all the 'bobby socks' – the girls – would be there and the old man would be, 'Come on, he's got a wife and kid at home and we've got to catch the 7.20 train.'

Harris felt no such compunction. Godwin knew of three mistresses that Harris kept in London alone.

Godwin went on to became the first paid British national cycling coach, and died shortly after the London 2012 Games, aged 91. Before an ill-fated move into business, Harris decided to retire from cycling in 1957. A fitting farewell was a two-centre series with his arch-rival, van Vliet – first in Amsterdam then at Herne Hill. The Meeting of Champions event, under the patronage of HM Queen Elizabeth at the south London venue, sold out despite the September chill. Both riders thrilled the crowd, and followed the script: Harris won three of the four races.

Track sprinting aside, cycling in Britain in the 1950s was on the whole an amateur sport. It was also mostly working class – an escape from the tedium of factories and offices. 'The roads were for cycling; you hardly ever saw a car,' said Tony Hoar, a professional cyclist in the 1950s, interviewed by Ellis Bacon for *Great British Cycling*. 'And the clubs! It was a really good time for cycling – probably the best there's ever been.' The staple of cycle clubs was the hard-riding Sunday run: all-day epics covering massive distances with stops for lunch and tea. Few concessions were made to younger members or novices – they held on to the pack for as long as they could and would then carry on solo – catching up with the group at lunch or heading home alone.

Hoar raced almost every day. 'You could, back then,' he continues:

> " There were mid-week time trials, and lots of circuit races. And then there was all the track racing, at Gosport, Portsmouth, Southampton, Poole Park and Brighton. That's one [Brighton] from the old penny-farthing days, with its little bit of banking on the last corner. Whoever designed it didn't know what the hell they were doing! "

One of the top clubs in the post-war period was the Norwood Paragon, formed in 1904 and boasting such luminaries as Frank Southall in the 1920s and 1930s, but then losing its way slightly, until a fresh crop of riders came through in the late 1940s. When Wally Happy, a road racer and aspiring track rider, joined the club in 1951 he was told that 'we ride everything in this club and the only condition is that we are always expected to finish in the first three' – be it track, road, time trial, grass or rollers. Happy went on to enjoy success on the track including winning the national team pursuit. He remembers:

> When I completed national service I couldn't get a decent paying job in civvy street, so I fitted a fixed-gear to my Hercules, took the brakes off and only raced the track for three years – attracted by the better prize money in that arena. In 1956, when we won the national team pursuit again, I remember earning £440 as a dental technician and £360 as a racing cyclist.

In 1955 the CurAcho Company sponsored the Golden Wheel pursuit trophy at the Good Friday Meeting for a second time (the first trophy having been won outright after three wins): it was won by Norman Sheil, an amateur endurance rider from Liverpool, of slight build with dark hair in a Tintin quiff. He went on to become world pursuit champion later in the year – and then won the Golden Wheel pursuit in the two following years, making the trophy his property and meaning CurAcho had to put their hand into their pocket yet again. Sheil also won the world pursuit championship again in 1958 and then switched to ride on the road in Europe, competing in the Tour de France in 1960.

Not everything Norwood Paragon did was met with unequivocal praise. The report in *Cycling* magazine on the

1956 Meeting of Champions praised their ability as team pursuit champions, but added:

> We must be frank about Saturday's thirty-eighth season-closing NCU Meeting of Champions at Herne Hill. The racing was fair, apart from the excess of it and the long-winded composition of a woman's sprint ... But the organization! It was just not good enough. Rarely have I seen it so crowded – with children abounding! A shilling programme full of literal errors and incomplete or sloppy information. No National Anthem at 3pm as indicated (the Queen gave the meeting her patronage), because the NCU's record was left in Denmark. "

Over in mainland Europe in the 1950s, cycling was still defined by professionals riding bunched road races, which dominated the local landscape and calendar in places like Flanders, northern France, the Basque country, northern Italy and Tuscany. But by 1957 the rules around the different branches and classes of racing in the UK gradually relaxed. First the National Cyclists' Union dropped its ban on British League of Racing Cyclists riders in 1953, then allowed amateurs and independents to mix in 1957. The Road Time Trials Council bizarrely agreed not to ban amateurs who had raced against independents, while still not allowing the two to race together under RTTC rules.

The NCU and BLRC did finally, grudgingly combine to

form the British Cycling Federation in 1959. The BLRC mod-
elled their UK races on the European ones. The riders raced
in short-sleeved cycling tops, shorts and white ankle socks,
and wore little cycling casquette caps and crochet-backed
track mitts. On training rides they wore plus-fours with
long patterned woollen socks and cycling-specific jumpers,
sometimes topped off with a black beret. Young riders were
becoming hooked by the Continental style.

There was huge interest at the time in the international stars
of the Grand Tours and one-day Classics, like Milan–San
Remo, Paris–Roubaix and La Flèche Wallonne. Few names
before or since were bigger than the great Fausto Coppi. He
was widely considered the finest, most elegant cyclist in the
history of the sport, winning the Tour de France twice and the
Giro d'Italia five times, and scores of one-day Classics, time
trials and track races. He was one of the great champions,
during one of cycling's great eras.

In an interview in *CycleSport Magazine*, Raphaël
Geminiani, a French teammate of Coppi and later a direc-
teur sportif, said:

> When Fausto won and you wanted to check the time
> gap to the man in second place, you didn't need a
> Swiss stopwatch. The bell of the church clock
> tower would do the job just as well. Paris–Roubaix?
> Milan–San Remo? Lombardy? We're talking

10 minutes to a quarter of an hour. That's how Fausto Coppi was. ""

So it was an audacious idea to bring Il Campionissimo – the 'Champion of Champions' – to Herne Hill, and guaranteed to generate interest beyond the usual track fans and club men across the country. Little matter that he was some way past his glorious best.

Keith Robins, who managed Herne Hill at the time, and promoted countless events there and elsewhere over a long career, was a canny and well-connected promoter. Having brought great crowds to Reg Harris's retirement meeting in September 1957, despite the waning popularity of track racing, he realised it was the names that brought the crowds. And big crowds brought big money, which in turn allowed big ambitions.

In late 1957 Robins spoke to Italo Berigliano, who owned the Beriano bike shop in Fulham, of his desire to bring international road men over to London. Coppi, for instance, would fill the stadium. A few months later Berigliano had planned a trip to Italy and asked Robins if he was still interested. 'Not half!' was the response. Although by that stage Robins was no longer manager at the track, he was still an active cycling promoter. While in Italy, Berigliano asked his good friend the sprinter Enzo Sacchi, gold medallist in the 1,000-metre sprint at the 1952 Helsinki Olympics, whether he could persuade Coppi to come to a meeting in London.

Berigliano returned from Italy in the middle of July with the news that Coppi, who had never raced in the UK before, could come on 14 September. And he would do so for a third of his usual fee. Coppi had a hectic end-of-season schedule; it was that day or never. They had two months to work out the programme.

Robins swiftly rang Charles King at the NCU, who had the lease on the track, and casually enquired whether he could hire the track 'for a VC Sacchi club meeting'. He paid an appropriate deposit and got a signed contract, just in time to announce in the *Evening Standard*: 'Coppi comes to London!' Charles King was on the phone by nine o'clock the next morning, saying he thought it was only a club meeting. Robins replied that it was, but Enzo Sacchi the club's president was bringing a couple of riders with him – one being his good friend Fausto Coppi.

The main problem was that 14 September was a Sunday, and The Lord's Day Observance Society would not permit charging the general public for events on a Sunday – although it was acceptable to charge members of a club, and so they hatched a plan. VC Sacchi, a small and relatively new racing club, which was based in Berigliano's bike shop, set up a Sunday club, which also entitled members to come to Sunday meetings. The VC Sacchi Sunday Club swiftly grew to over 12,000 members!

The programme was quickly pulled together, with Coppi being joined by fellow Italians Sacchi, Nino Defilippis, a road racer who won the Giro di Lombardia in 1958, as well as numerous Grand Tour stages, and Elmo Pesenti, the Italian sprint champion.

They were matched against four professionals from 'the rest of the world': there was Brian Robinson, the first Englishman ever to finish the Tour de France, in 1955 (but only just – Tony Hoar finished the same Tour in 69th and final place, taking the Lanterne Rouge), an achievement he capped a few months before the Coppi meeting by becoming the first ever English winner of a stage; and Seamus 'Shay' Elliott the young Irish road racer, who was already making a mark in continental Europe and would go on to win stages in all the Grand Tours, becoming the first Irishman to wear the yellow jersey in the Tour de France (1963) and coming third in the 1962 Vuelta a España.

They in turn were joined by two Australians: sprinter John Tresidder, national sprint champion in 1951 and second in the world sprint championships in 1954; and Roger Arnold, who had made his name as a six-day man, but was also a top sprinter, omnium rider, pursuiter and derny racer.

Top road men, cooed Berigliano in the programme: 'the glamour boys of professional cycle racing'. They weren't dyed-in-the-wool 'track men', but they could all certainly ride the track. Mark Cavendish believes the UCI (the Union Cycliste Internationale – the world governing body for the sport of cycling) has made it almost impossible for cyclists to combine the track and road nowadays. 'The UCI has segregated track and road cycling completely,' he said in 2015. 'It's killing track cycling, because you never get the road stars doing track anymore. Track cycling is going to die, particularly on the endurance side. There's just no way to qualify without quitting the road.'

But back in 1958 Robins wanted to ensure a real show and pulled together a roster of 30 of the best amateur track men in the country too, all under contract to ride, so the full programme included four amateur distance races interspersed with the professional showcase. Each amateur also had his own mechanic to see to his needs.

It was going to be one of the biggest, most ambitious track meetings for years. Berigliano got sponsorship for pretty much everything, in particular drawing on his links with the pillars of London's Italian expat community such as Bianchi's and Pinocchio restaurants in Soho, Bertorelli Bros restaurant on Charlotte Street and the Mazzini-Garibaldi Club in Clerkenwell, not to mention national icons Gaggia, Martini & Rossi, Cinzano and Lambretta.

In the 1950s there was practically no TV or newspaper coverage of any cycling events, and most people could only read about the cycling stars in magazines bought in the Italian areas of London such as Soho and Clerkenwell, where there was great enthusiasm for cycling. But word soon spread, with seemingly the whole of London's Italian expatriate community planning to attend. Italian restaurants in London were closed on Sundays, so all Italian waiters were free to see their idol, Coppi. But so too were local club members. Go to any veterans' meeting nowadays and most old hands still claim: 'I was there.'

Most fans went to the shop in Fulham to join VC Sacchi and buy tickets. Others who left it late paid to go to the Meeting of Champions event at Herne Hill on Saturday 13 September, just so they could go to Berigliano's stand to buy tickets for the next day. A typical meeting at Herne Hill in the late 1950s was two shillings to stand on the terrace, but the Coppi meeting cost five shillings to join VC Sacchi and attend the meeting. And yet there were 11,000–12,000 spectators on the day paying to see Coppi.

As Jock Wadley, editor of *Sporting Cyclist*, wrote in his programme foreword:

> 66 He is 39 tomorrow, and on the track today we do not expect to see miracles and record-breaking performances. But, as a man who has always given of his best throughout his great career, we shall catch glimpses of the supreme Coppi. We shall see those thousands of familiar photographs leaping to life as he laps our famous track – a track that has borne the wheel of many champions, but today receives Il Campionissimo, the champion of champions. 99

Sunday 14 September 1958 was a sunny and windless day, perfect for racing. By the time the gates opened at noon, queues had formed all the way down Burbage Road. Coppi only arrived in London on the Sunday morning, disappointing the expectant guests at a hastily arranged party the night before at Pinocchio's restaurant on Frith Street in Soho. He was scheduled to arrive on a 9am flight on the Sunday morning, but Robins, who had just had his first telephone installed at home, received his first phone call at 2am. It was a telephonist from London Airport (as Heathrow was known in those days) saying a 'Mr Coppi wants to know which hotel he's staying at'. He was pointed in the direction of the Dorchester Hotel with his bike.

To entertain the crowds before the main programme began there were record attempts on the 1-mile and 5-mile standing-start tandem race by Mike Gambrill, bronze medallist in the team pursuit at the 1956 Olympics, and his younger brother Robin. They narrowly failed at 1 mile, but smashed the 5-mile record. The younger brother, on the back, threw his helmet into the crowd in celebration. The crowd's anticipation was growing.

The centre of the track was then cleared of everyone other than officials, ready for a 3pm start. At 2.45 the Italian priest of St Patrick's Roman Catholic Church in Soho blessed the crowd from the grandstand steps and they sang the Italian national anthem. Then all the amateurs came on in a grand procession. As they were introduced, each rode one lap around the top of the track with a bouquet of flowers, then dropped to the inside line and kept on riding: 15 yards between each of them in a perfectly choreographed show.

The stars then warmed up to cheering and tumultuous clapping. Each professional was introduced and rode a solo lap before dropping into the track centre and getting off his bike. Coppi, the last to arrive, was greeted with rapturous applause. When he too had finished his lap and rode into the track centre, a gun was fired and the amateurs rode up to the rails and threw their bouquets into the wild crowd.

The first event was the 500-metre sprint between the stereotypical-looking Italian rider Sacchi and Tresidder, with tightly curled black hair, a low hairline and a broad face. After a cautious stand-off 20 yards from the start, Sacchi made the first move of the day and soon Tresidder was trailing by five yards, only to come off the final banking like a rocket past Sacchi. But the Italian fought back to catch Tresidder 20 yards from the line to win by 'a gnat's whisker' according to *The Racing Cyclist* reporter. Arnold faced Pesenti in the second sprint, with Pesenti sitting on Arnold's wheel until he made a final move to clinch it – by no more than a tyre this time.

The third event was a 5-kilometre double-harness pursuit (a pursuit raced by pairs, madison-style), Coppi making his first appearance on the track, with Defilippis, facing Robinson and Elliott. 'Coppi, Coppi' was bellowed from one half of the track while the other half cheered the English-speaking pair. It was a fast start, with Robinson and Elliott taking an early lead and maintaining 15–20 yards of air for the first six laps, but then Coppi started to get into his stride. With four laps to go they were level and the ground was in uproar. They fought shoulder to shoulder for the next few laps, but by the bell Coppi and Defilippis had opened up a 10-yard gap which the other pair were unable to close down.

Thirty of the best amateurs in England then contested

the 5-mile points race with a 'devilishly fast' pace – Mike Gambrill won again, but in third place was a certain Tom Simpson, who went on to become one of Britain's most successful, iconic and tragic professional cyclists.

The next two events were 700-metre sprints: first between Tresidder and Pesenti, in 'an all-out, ding-dong battle all the way' with Tresidder taking it on the home straight; then Sacchi faced Arnold, a veteran of Herne Hill. This time it was a slow, tactical race with Arnold keeping Sacchi high on the track, but with 220 metres to go Sacchi stole the lead and held it to the line by half a wheel.

All four road men featured in the next race, the 1,000-metre sprint. Coppi smiled wryly to the crowd as he led the snaking, showboating quartet past the grandstand before the bell, but it ultimately ended with the four side-by-side down the home straight, finishing Robinson, Defilippis, Elliott, Coppi. It was a perfect racing spectacle and the crowd were lapping it up, despite their hero's obvious decline since his days of pomp. The professionals had a contract and earned a fee to race: they were riding for entertainment, not prizes. Their job on days like this was to keep the crowd happy.

And the crowd were very happy in their shirtsleeves on a wonderful, sunny Italian Sunday. The air was fragrant with the smell of eau de cologne from the Italian fans. Ice creams were in abundance, as well as the usual crusty rolls. And there was non-stop music, most appropriately the song that defined the summer of 1958: *Volare*, that year's Italian entry to the Eurovision Song Contest, by singer-songwriter Domenico

Modugno, and well on its way to selling more than 22 million copies worldwide, making it one of the most popular Eurovision songs of all time.

'I just remember the noise,' says Brenda Robins, wife of Keith and a keen amateur cyclist herself. 'The crowd cheered absolutely everything.' The presentation was smooth and slick too – the mechanics were encouraged by the great prizes on offer for the amateurs to get their men quickly into pole position for the start of each race – and halfway through the meeting they were 20 minutes ahead of schedule. So they had a break, with the professionals riding around the track, giving autographs and posing for photographs.

The next event was a 6-kilometre points race for the professional road men. It was a fast start, with Robinson and Defilippis sharing the first couple of laps, then Elliott took three of the next five, with Robinson keeping two. But then Elliott and Defilippis started to drop way back and Il Campionissimo asserted himself, taking three of the next four laps off Robinson. They almost lapped the other two, only to fall back again, but as the bell went Robinson surged ahead past the battling Coppi to win by three lengths with 42 points – eight points clear of Coppi.

By now the heat was oppressive and the four track men were sweating heavily as they lined up for the next 1,000-metre sprint. The Italians led by the bell and all four were predictably in the mix at the highly orchestrated finish, but Pesenti produced his trademark kick and won by a tyre's width from Tresidder, with Sacchi only half a wheel behind.

After the amateur Devil (also known as the Devil-take-the-hindmost or Elimination race, where a rider or two are eliminated each lap, leaving a few to race for the line at the finish), the grand finale was signalled by the muscular, throaty chugging and blue smoke of eight Lambrettas warming up in the centre of the track. Twenty-two laps, 10 kilometres, at over 30mph, being paced at close quarters by the iconic scooters brought in for the Italian festival of speed. Coppi took an early lead after the Lambrettas picked up their riders, but then Elliott took over and held on for lap after lap, as the others vied for places. Arnold attacked on lap six, fighting with Pesenti and Coppi, eventually moving into third. Robinson slowed down and Sacchi dropped out. He attacked again on lap fourteen, trying to take Elliott on the back straight, but failed. Pesenti dropped out, and with seven laps to go Arnold finally took the lead. With four laps to go Coppi attacked, but Arnold held on despite a fierce finish, with Elliott and Coppi taking second and third places.

The final result was 'the rest of the world' on 28 points, beating the Italians by a single point. It was a brilliant display of racing, which kept the crowd thoroughly entertained. Lord Donegal presented the prizes with the Italian Vice-Consul, to rapturous applause from one of the largest attendances since the Second World War. Ercole Baldini, the 1956 Olympic gold medallist at individual pursuit who went on to win the world professional road race title and the Giro d'Italia in 1958, visited in April 1959 and Coppi came back in September 1959, but the crowds were smaller – Coppi's first visit had been a swansong.

In the meantime, Coppi had to fight through the crowds swarming around the entrance to the changing rooms underneath the grandstand, then rush off to catch an evening flight from the airport: he had contracts to race elsewhere.

8

# Pop goes the track

The late 1950s and the 1960s were largely prosperous years, part of the post-war boom about which prime minister Harold Macmillan said Britons had 'never had it so good'. Consumer spending grew, especially on durables such as cars, TVs and washing machines; there was a much wider and more sophisticated variety of mass entertainment available to everyone. There was also the expansion of secondary and tertiary education, the rise of white collar employment and the growth of the middle class.

Such improvements in economic and social conditions contributed in part to the waning popularity of cycling in the face of so many alternative temptations. Roger St Pierre, a cycling journalist, pins the post-war decline of cycling to 1959: the year the first Mini was produced. Greater disposable income, combined with small, cheap and very cool little cars, transformed young people's attitude towards cycling. 'Growing up, you had a pair of roller skates, then a bike, then a cheap motorbike and then a car, but all of a sudden that middle chunk was taken away,' St Pierre said. In the 1950s everyone rode a bike to work; by the mid-1960s cycling to the factory was seen as a sign of 'being a pleb'.

The situation was also looking increasingly grim for Herne Hill track: the British Cycling Federation, the new national governing body for cycle racing that had superseded the National Cyclists' Union, didn't have sufficient funds or staff to maintain the grounds. In 1958 London County Council had shown an interest in the stadium and was sympathetic about safeguarding the facility. A report from the Parks Department in October 1959 talked of the 'grave danger that this well-established centre of sport in South London might soon be wholly lost' and outlined a plan to repair and extend the facilities, to provide still greater value to the public in future. Fortunately London County Council took on the lease from landowners the Dulwich Estate, for a period of 42 years.

This marked a new direction for Herne Hill: taking on a broader role as a community facility. By 1965, when the Greater London Council (GLC) replaced London County Council, the use of the athletics track, especially by schools, had increased considerably, with over 10,000 schoolchildren using it each year. The newly formed Inner London Education Authority (ILEA) Cycling Education Centre was part of a wider movement throughout the country to raise interest and participation in sport.

The Central Council for Physical Recreation, an advisory organisation (which eventually gave birth to the Sports Council), was also set up at this time, in part as a response to the domination of Iron Curtain countries which were heavily 'subsidising' Olympic sports and seeing the results in terms of medals. A youth programme of cycling at Herne Hill was kicked off under the guidance of full-time coaches Shaun Purcell, Bill Dodds and Dave Creasey. It included sessions for local schools, Friday night youth training and hugely popular holiday clubs.

The coaches were a tough bunch who took no nonsense. One schoolboy from Wandsworth Comprehensive who used to go there every week for a games lesson recalls the coach's opening words at the first session: 'If I see any dangerous messing about, I will ride out and put you over the barriers.'

Dave Creasey was always at his best when coaching youngsters, taking anyone who showed an interest under his wing. One such protégé was John Scripps, who began training with him in the 1990s and became a close friend. Scripps says:

> He was always completely serious about the whole sport. It was never something he would take lightly. But he was brutal as a coach. He would stand there with his megaphone and literally scream and shout across the track.

Woe betide anyone who committed an infringement.

Another big character at the time was Eddie Wingrave, who had a reputation for being the most vicious sports official you could ever hope to meet. If anyone took their hands off the handlebars for a victory salute, they were immediately disqualified – as Bradley Wiggins later found out to his cost. At Wingrave's funeral someone apparently quipped: 'I'm glad the pallbearers kept their hands on the bars!'

'Dave [Creasey] would come and go and never ask for any thanks or recognition,' says Scripps, who after working as a British Cycling coach for a number of years himself is now operations manager at Lee Valley VeloPark. 'People like him, Ron Fowler, Ron Beckett, Eddie Wingrave, these stalwarts were flawed characters in some respects, but they did it for complete selfless love of the sport.'

Steve Cave, who came through the youth programme, recalls his boyhood at the track fondly. His first experience of Herne Hill, as for many others, was the holiday club. Having cycled twelve miles to the track each day as a fourteen-year-old, he would be coached by Dave Creasey and Shaun Purcell. That's where he learned how to race. 'It was the same then as it is now,' he says. 'You'd start on the track as a youngster, but as you got older you'd move towards the road.'

'Everyone rode the track,' says Cave.

> Whether you were good at it or not, you rode the track to gain speed, to hone your skills and that's how they became top road men. If you're in a bunch of 140 riders how do you get out? You need to swing the bike to get in position and that's the sort of thing you learn at the track.

He recalls the park-keeper, who managed the facility but never went near a bike himself, sitting in a smoky little office around the back of the grandstand, wearing a brown GLC work uniform. In traditional 'parky' manner, he would chase pesky kids who climbed over the fence and ran across the cricket grounds for a shortcut to the chip shop, 'banning' them from the track. Outside of organised sessions riders had to pay him to go on the track – or slip him a bottle of beer.

The initiative certainly achieved its objective of nurturing a new generation of racing cyclists – such as Maurice Burton, who went on to become the first black British rider to successfully break into the Continental six-day scene, and, later, Russell Williams who went on to win the national derny championship – but the wider cycling community took time to catch up.

Most cycle clubs still didn't admit under-18s at this time, due to the lack of supervision that could be offered to youngsters, and even when they hit adulthood they could only get into a club if a parent or relative proposed them for membership. At Herne Hill, there was no under-14 racing until it was introduced in 1968. Norwood Paragon CC didn't admit under-15s until 1985 – or women for that matter! The solution was a new club affiliated to the British Cycling Federation to cater for boys and girls who had been through the ILEA Cycling Education Centre: Velo Club Londres (VCL) was set up in 1964 by Shaun Purcell and Bill Dodds, with the aim of encouraging young riders into the sport.

Such positive news couldn't disguise the greater malaise,

however: Britain's role in international competitive cycling was declining. The flagship track event at Herne Hill, the Meeting of Champions, was unable to survive. Run every year since 1908, with the exception of war years, it stopped running in 1965. Velodromes in strongholds such as France, Belgium and Italy were experiencing similar fates due to the prevailing socio-economic and cultural trends, but those in Britain suffered additional competition from the rising popularity of road racing.

The situation in the UK had turned full circle from the 1890s when cyclists had been forced by the National Cyclists' Union to abandon road racing and hold their events on tracks or closed circuits: by the 1960s the British Cycling Federation had given the green light to road racing. There was an explosion in the popularity of Continental professional road racing, with superstar road men such as Eddy Merckx – widely thought to be the greatest and most successful rider in the history of cycling – and emerging home-grown superstars such as Tom Simpson.

Simpson was one of Britain's most successful professional cyclists. Born in County Durham and raised in Nottinghamshire, he began road cycling as a teenager before taking up track cycling, specialising in pursuit races. He won a bronze medal in the team pursuit at the 1956 Olympics in Melbourne and a silver at the 1958 British Empire and Commonwealth Games in the individual pursuit. Simpson rode one of his final amateur races at the Good Friday Meeting in 1959. The mid-1950s had seen a revival in motor-paced racing, with many motors and riders coming from behind the Iron Curtain where it had remained popular. Simpson led the race in typically courageous fashion against some leading Eastern Bloc racers, until he blew up eleven laps from the end of a 70-lap race, leaving world motor-paced champion Lothar Meister from East Germany to roar through victorious.

When he turned professional in July 1959, Simpson rapidly became every English cyclist's idol as he took the continental European road race scene by storm, with a reputation as a courageous, attacking rider. In 1960 he rode the Tour de France in the GB team (the Tour still featured national, rather than trade teams), with Brian Robinson and Norman Sheil. In 1961 he won the Tour of Flanders (one of the five one-day Classic Monuments); in 1962 he became the first British rider to wear the yellow jersey in the Tour de France, before finishing sixth overall; in 1963 he won Bordeaux–Paris; and in 1964 he won Milan–San Remo. More was still to come: he was the most famous, successful and soon-to-be notorious English cyclist of his generation.

It wasn't simply a case of allegiances transferring from the track to the peloton, however; fortunately many of the road men loved to ride track too. And it was appearances at Herne Hill by stars such as Simpson and Barry Hoban that provided many of the highlights of the 1960s. Hoban was a few years younger than Simpson but inspired by the European successes of Simpson and Robinson he went to France in 1962, then turned professional two years later, winning two stages of the 1964 Vuelta a España. Hoban was like Simpson – a track rider first and foremost, with a rapid sprint and a shrewd racing brain. He was the other big character of the 1960s British racing scene.

Hoban went on to hold the record for the most stage wins in the Tour de France by a British rider, winning eight between 1967 and 1975, and was also the only Briton to have won two consecutive stages of the Tour until things changed for British cycling in the 21st century. He still holds the record for the most Tours completed by a British rider, having finished eleven of the twelve he started between 1965 and 1978.

In those years when Simpson appeared at Good Friday Meetings in the early to mid-1960s the gates were up by 50 per cent or more. His victory in the Tour of Flanders just two weeks before his first Good Friday Meeting in 1961 made him a national hero, and he went on to win the pursuit against Johannes de Haan, winner of the previous season's autumn Classic, the Paris–Tours.

In the early 1960s, Keith Waldegrave was by his own admission 'a spotty, adolescent, teenage time triallist and a member of the Ashford Wheelers Cycling Club in Kent'. The Wheelers held 10-mile time trials on Wednesday evenings. They raced in 25- and 50-mile time trials on Sunday mornings, rode club runs in the afternoon and took part in midweek evening chain gangs around the Kent country lanes. They did all this on fixed-wheel bikes on 69-inch or 72-inch gears depending on the time of year, and generally raced on 81-inch or 84-inch gears in time trials. In 1962, aged seventeen, Waldegrave and a group from the club rode the 120-mile return day trip to Herne Hill for the Good Friday Meeting, a serious workout on fixed wheels.

One year on, and Waldegrave's enthusiasm for the heroics of Jacques Anquetil and Simpson was eclipsed by a growing interest in photography, as he became a trainee photographer with the *Kentish Express*. The local weekly paper provided a Speed Graphic plate camera – a truly cumbersome piece of kit. Only five plates remain from the 1963 meeting, but from his vantage point at the start of the home straight looking back at the banking they show Simpson in the familiar iconic black and white Peugeot BP jersey engaged in derny-paced racing against Hoban, Paul de Paepe of Belgium (winner of the world motor-paced championship in 1957), Australian Roger Arnold making his last appearance in Europe and Leo Proost of Belgium (who would go on to win the world motor-paced championships three times). The race also featured Alf Engers, the brilliant London-born maverick rider who set numerous national records and won national individual time trial championships, and who had made a name for himself with a notable win in the CurAcho Golden Wheel trophy at Good Friday 1960 as a precocious 20-year-old.

Having gone on to spend over 50 years as a press photographer, Waldegrave now lives less than a mile from Herne Hill Velodrome, and still rides his steel Ron Cooper track bike at the Wednesday morning veterans' sessions, where he has a mean sprint.

At the 1964 Good Friday Meeting, fresh from his triumph

in the Milan–San Remo, Simpson was in a tightly fought omnium against Emil Severens, Leon Franssen, John Geddes, John Woodburn and Alf Engers again. Simpson won, but was pressed hard by Engers. A year on, Simpson became Britain's first world road race champion and won the Giro di Lombardia; this made him the BBC Sports Personality of the Year for 1965, the first cyclist to win the award. He attributed his victory over Rudi Altig in the world championship to track craft. Holding the German's wheel, he switched sides to take his run for the line. Altig glanced back the wrong way and, in that moment of hesitation, Simpson had the advantage. He should have made lots of money after winning the world championship, but breaking his leg in a ski accident put paid to that.

The following Good Friday Meeting saw Jiri Daler from Czechoslovakia, the 1964 Olympic pursuit champion, who would go on to win the CurAcho Pursuit trophy three times, but he met his match in 1966 when facing Hugh 'the Locomotive' Porter, from Wolverhampton: a tall, lean rider with brown hair and a long face. Having won the British national track championship pursuit title three years on the trot from 1963 to 1965, Porter went into the meeting brimming with confidence. Porter and Daler met in the first heat, which should really have been the final – Daler took an early lead but Porter slowly pulled back to finish half a wheel ahead at the 4,000-metres finish.

Porter turned professional the next year and went on to become one of Britain's greatest-ever professional cyclists, winning four world titles in the individual pursuit in the late 1960s and early 1970s.

Given that he was at the peak of his career and a massive draw for crowds when he returned to racing after his leg had healed, Simpson demanded that the home professionals riding against him let him win, reports Les Woodland. Dave Bonner, a south Londoner, disagreed and beat him. 'He told me I should let him win, that he was the one the people had come to see,' Bonner said. 'I told him to beat me if he could. He wasn't happy.' Fixing races was no novelty for Simpson, who used to ride the Continental six-days wearing a bowler hat and carrying an umbrella – 'Major Tom'. He was one of the best six-day riders of the time, loved for his clowning and flashy shows of skill. When he was racing, Simpson would sometimes ride up the advertising boards at the top of the bankings, Wall of Death-style, to please the crowds.

During the 1960s and 1970s, six-day races were held successfully at Wembley and sponsored by the brewers of Skol lager. A forerunner to these events was held at Earl's Court in September 1967 on a tiny prefabricated track with very steep 50-degree banking, and was meant to be a showcase for Simpson, partnering Ron Baensch. Simpson had announced to the press his intention of giving up the road in favour of specialising on the lucrative winter track circuit, but instead of making six-day racing his new career, fate had something else in store for him.

Having won the Paris–Nice and two stages of the Vuelta in 1967, he went into the Tour with high hopes. But on the thirteenth stage, Simpson collapsed and died during the ascent of Mont Ventoux, the 'Beast of Provence'. But it wasn't the mountain that killed him: he had mixed amphetamines and alcohol, which proved fatal when combined with the intense heat, the hard climb of Ventoux and a stomach complaint. Simpson was widely known to have taken performance-enhancing drugs during his career; doping was 'hidden' but no controls existed. His death was a tragic sign of the times.

New cycle tracks were built in Welwyn in 1960 and Leicester in 1967, in time for the 1970 world championship – the first time Britain had hosted the event since 1904, when Leon Meredith had been in his pomp. Both tracks had steeper banking and were reputed to be faster than Herne Hill, and they took yet more racing away from the south London venue.

In 1969 the *News of the World* ended their 21-year association with the Good Friday Meeting and by the early 1970s it was no longer an international event. From 1973 all the major national track championships were held in Leicester – Herne Hill was no longer the centre of British track cycling.

Despite some success at the 1970 world championships in Leicester (gold for Hugh Porter in the professional pursuit, silver for Ian Hallam in the amateur pursuit and bronze for Beryl Burton in the women's pursuit), by the early 1970s track cycling barely existed as a spectator sport, such was the rapid decline. Herne Hill was only attracting a few hundred spectators – down from the heady days of 10,000 only a decade earlier. A sad reminder of the decline came in 1971, when Reg Harris came out of his fourteen-year retirement to take bronze in the British professional sprint championship; and then again in 1974 he took the British title – aged 54! By that time professional sprinting was clearly a shadow of what it had been.

Alf Engers was dominating short-distance time trials in the early 1970s, turning the race format into a spectator sport. He used 'marginal gains', some 25 years before Dave Brailsford introduced the transformational concept. Engers trimmed, shaved and drilled holes in his bikes to make them as light as possible, hiding brakes and brake levers from the air flow and using extra-thin track tyres. He wore a silk track jersey tucked into silk shorts, with patent leather shoes, and taped down the laces for greater aerodynamics.

Engers had a rock star persona, with long frizzy hair and Afghan coats, hippy t-shirts and wide flares. In interviews he talked about meditation and carp fishing. He was disdainful of officials, they were disdainful of him, and in 1971 he was in the middle of one of his many disputes with officialdom, so his appearance in the Roadman's Pursuit at Herne Hill was watched with keen interest. The Roadman's Pursuit has competitors at intervals around the track starting simultaneously, attempting to catch and therefore eliminate the rider in front within the ten-minute time limit. Engers was inspired that day, and crushed the opposition, with only three riders remaining on the track at the finish. His closest rival was

Ray Ward, over 300 yards back. Engers won again in 1974 and 1976. In 1976 only one rider survived the onslaught – the seventeen-year-old Tony Doyle, who went on to win the following year. In 1979 Sean Yates, yet another promising youth, won the Campagnola trophy (CurAcho had stopped their sponsorship of the Good Friday Meeting pursuit after 20 years, to be replaced by the Italian cycle components manufacturer).

But despite nascent success on the road from Simpson, Hoban, Robinson and a few other pioneers, Britain had hit a dry patch in track cycling. There were world champions every few years, from Norman Sheil in 1955 and 1958 through to Hugh Porter in 1968, 1970, 1972 and 1973, but no Olympic track medals throughout the entire 1960s (and only two bronze for team pursuit in the 1950s). When Sheil took control of the track team in 1971, things started to look up, starting with a bronze medal for the team pursuit in the Munich Olympics in 1972, followed by silver in the team pursuit in 1973 at the San Sebastian world championships. 'Now that's a successful team,' he said. But it was, of course, nothing compared to what was to come 20 years later.

There was still exciting racing at Herne Hill for the stalwarts, but by the late 1970s and into the 1980s attendances were declining even further, sponsorship was rare and cycling was very much viewed as a fringe activity. Good Friday Meetings had still enjoyed 6,000-odd spectators in 1960, but this fell to 3,000–4,000 visitors in the 1980s.

While the root cause of the decline of cycling as a

national pastime and dominant cultural force was doubtless related to the socio-economic transformation in the 1950s and 1960s, it doesn't fully explain the drastic decline of public interest in track racing specifically. In theory the same factors would cause a decline in interest in road racing, yet if anything it actually became more popular. The bright, brash colours of the peloton, nip and tuck of tactics, adrenalin rush of the power sprint finish and the death-or-glory heroics of the breakaway wooed fans, media and sponsors alike.

Track cycling, however, seemed to be becoming more sanitised – at least as far as the spectators were concerned. There was a gradual transition towards race formats designed to test individual athletic prowess, rather than entertain the crowds. So pursuits and time trials remained, while tandem racing and motor-paced events died away and bunch races were less common. Thriving local competitive scenes were gradually eroded, grass-track racing and village fete meetings died out, and handicap races, which gave local amateurs cause for hope, disappeared from programmes. And the big personalities that entertained the crowds with clowning and showmanship on the track, fuelled by feuds and rivalries both on and off it, were in short supply – or had simply moved to the European road circuit.

In the late 1970s, Graham Bristow was an average club rider with a preference for track sprinting, whose family was steeped in bike racing and Herne Hill in particular. He was born in

1949 and family folklore had it that he had most probably been conceived at the track during the 1948 Olympics – presumably on Lovers' Walk. He still has photos of his mother riding on the track when she was three months pregnant with him. The family used to watch all the big meetings and when Bristow left school at sixteen in the summer of 1965 his dad took him up to Herne Hill and introduced him to the resident coach, before enrolling him in the holiday club (a six-week intensive course in race craft), before starting work.

He rode regularly through the late 1960s and 1970s on road and track, but in 1978 his club, Norwood Paragon, was in need of a new organiser for the Champagne Meeting, sponsored by Moet & Chandon since 1971, so Bristow stopped racing and took on the job. It was the start of a long involvement in race promotion that continues through to today, as organiser of the Good Friday Meetings. At the end of that first midweek evening, the final reckoning showed that 1,500 people had come through the gates and Bristow was hooked: 'I got such a buzz out of it.'

He continued to organise the meeting, taking it from a Wednesday evening fixture to a Saturday as success grew and they could attract more riders from 'up-country'. It was even a two-day weekend meeting for a while. One year a plane flew up from Biggin Hill and a parachutist dropped in with a huge blow-up champagne bottle. The *Daily Mirror* became joint sponsor of the meeting for 1986 and 1987, then pulled out leaving Moet as the main sponsor for 1988; but then they too stopped supporting the event. The meeting morphed into

The GP of London Meeting (named after the sprint race which had been held within the meeting since 1978), but with no sponsorship forthcoming the final meeting was held in 1990.

'There was lots and lots of racing,' says Peter Cattermole, a professional rider in his late teens and early twenties until his career was cut short by injury, who went on to become chairman of VC Londres and manage Herne Hill Velodrome:

> " There were periods when I was a youth when I raced 20 days on the trot ... I raced day after day. Monday at Herne Hill, Tuesday at Crystal Palace, Wednesday back at Herne Hill, Thursday league at Eastway, Friday at Sutcliffe Park, then some town centre races at the weekend. Then back to Herne Hill. "

Monday 'comp' at Herne Hill was still popular, but it was treated as a recovery ride for many after the weekend road races. Wednesday was the big event and the big guns would come out – the likes of Ron Keeble and Ian Hallam (both of whom went on to Olympic success in the team pursuit, among other honours). It was mainly amateurs racing at the weekly meetings, but the Champagne Meeting and Good Friday Meeting had the big money prizes on offer, so different riders would come along, including Continental professionals.

During this period good riders could still make a living out of track racing in Britain – just about. A decent rider

could earn a week's wage in one night. They could win a
month's money in one night if they went up to Leicester. 'The
prizes were very good,' continues Cattermole:

> When I got my first job I was getting £15–20/week, but
> I was making more than that cycling. Certainly when
> I was nineteen I'd be making reasonable money over
> here, but I would go to Holland for a week and come
> back with £200 in my pocket.

Bristow recalls a group of Australians who raced at Herne
Hill at this time, including Gary Wiggins (Bradley's father).
Wiggins had arrived in 1974 as Australian national junior
track champion and harbouring a fierce ambition to make a
name for himself. He joined the Archer Road Club, based in
west London and sponsored by Cutty Sark whisky, and was
soon part of an Antipodean scene including Dave and John
Sanders, Robin Croker, Steve Hefferman and Danny Clark,
who had won silver in the 1,000-metre time trial in the 1972
Olympics in Munich.

They were a notoriously tough bunch: Wiggins was well
known for using his fists with friends and enemies alike.
Cattermole recalls the Aussies turning up at Paddington track
with elbow pads for one race: 'we soon found out why'.

There was a lot of rough and tumble in the races – lots
of hooks and elbows – particularly in those with a mix of professionals and amateurs. Amateurs were a lot rougher than
professionals, who knew they needed to keep working. It was

common to be ridden into the rails on the track or into a ditch on the road races. 'It was fun then,' says Steve Cave, who by the late 1970s had joined the Nomads, a leading club in the south-east during this period.

> " It was a lot tougher. We were barging, we were hooking. You had to be able to cope with it or you'd hit the deck. You'd think you were going to win a race, you'd be going flat out and the next minute you'd be at the back, because someone had pulled your jersey. Normally it would be Ron Keeble! "

Keeble was a leading rider from the Nomads, the main rivals to the Archer Road Club. He was a big, brash, outspoken but likeable 'hard man' from the Elephant and Castle. He first came to prominence when he won the White Hope Sprint in 1966, going on to win his first national titles in 1969 and then a team pursuit bronze medal at the 1972 Munich Games alongside Mick Bennett, Ian Hallam and William Moore – although that victory was bittersweet as they could well have won gold if it weren't for a puncture in the semi-final against eventual winners West Germany. The Nomads also included Glen Mitchell, Dave Le Grys and Sean Yates, all of whom competed successfully at international level.

Ian Hallam, meanwhile, was winner of multiple national titles, three Commonwealth gold medals and two bronze, and went on to win a second Olympic bronze medal in team pursuit in Montreal in 1976. VC Londres was also beginning to produce some great riders. Maurice Burton, born in London to an English mother and a Jamaican father, was first drawn to cycling when he watched Eddy Merckx's 1969 Tour de France exploits in ten-minute slots on ITV's *World of Sport*. The following year Burton joined school trips to Herne Hill and was further inspired by the coaches he met there, in particular Bill Dodds. By 1973 he'd won the national junior sprint title, and the following year he won the White Hope Sprint at the Good Friday Meeting. He also won the 20-kilometre amateur scratch national title in August 1974, but as the first black British champion in cycling he was booed as he crossed the line.

The teenage 'Slow-Mo' had great tactical instincts, a tough personality and a formidable turn of speed. But he was frustrated by the racism in Britain at the time. Burton, with his school friend Joe Clovis, who came fourth in the 1973 junior sprint race, and Jim Robertson – who enjoyed less success, but remarkably has raced every season at Herne Hill from 1970 through to today – were the only three black riders at the track at the time. Clovis recalled his tyres frequently failing official inspections before races when all the white kids passed without comment. To prove the point, on one occasion he borrowed wheels that had just passed inspection from a white boy – on his bike they failed.

Inspired by the high levels of professionalism he saw in cycling in Belgium, Burton moved to Ghent, a major centre for Continental cycling. In 1977 he turned professional for the winter season, and he went on to ride 56 professional six-day events over eight seasons. He could earn £2,000 or more a week during the winter months – £35,000 a year showed that serious money could be earned on the 'Blue Train' – the lucrative elite of six-day racers.

Fellow VC Londres rider Russell Williams enjoyed sustained success on track and road as amateur and professional, from winning the national road race championships as a junior in 1978 through to winning the national derny championships in 2002, before starting a career as a Eurosport commentator. Unlike Burton he chose to stay local and even in his thirties he was still training at Herne Hill under the watchful eye of Dave Creasey.

In 1975, the seventeen-year-old Tony Doyle was also a regular at Herne Hill, riding every Monday and Wednesday meeting – any race from sprints to endurance. As he told Geoffrey Nicholson for his biography:

> The track sport was very healthy at that time. Even in the weekly meetings we'd get 150 competitors. On Wednesdays they'd come down from the Midlands and since that meeting was open to pros, you'd even get people like Tony Gowland [winner of the Skol 6 at Wembley three years before] turning up.

Gowland was the only Briton to win a London six-day event since the war. A red-haired, freckled man with a round face and a reputation for being a tough sprinter, he was paired with the even faster sprinter Patrick Sercu of Belgium in 1972.

Gowland had startled the field as an unknown rider at Herne
Hill a few years earlier by simply riding away from everyone.

Mick Bennett, who had enjoyed Olympic success in the
team pursuit in the early 1970s, and later turned professional
on road and track, also talked to Nicholson. He remembers
first coming across Doyle at a Herne Hill meeting when he
was still a junior. He was

> " a long, lanky lad, quite ungainly on the bike …
> He was in a break with Ian Hallam and me and we
> worked him over. But because he finished third, I
> know I went over afterwards to Harry Walker, the
> Welsh masseur who was managing the junior team,
> and said that he was going to be a good lad, Doyle. "

Doyle was indeed a good lad. He went on the become world
professional pursuit champion in 1980 and 1986, but also the
best six-day racer this country has ever produced, winning
23 events in his career. He ended up partnering two of the
London-based Aussies – Gary Wiggins and Danny Clark –
whose combative style and personality had led them to pursue
greater riches in Continental six-day racing. In early 1979
Wiggins had also moved to Ghent to pursue his dream. One
of his early Madison partners was Maurice Burton, and by
the early 1980s both Wiggins and Clark had forced their way
into the Blue Train.

The truly brutal regime of six-day racing at the beginning of the 20th century had gradually 'softened' through the

introduction of two-man teams, enabling riders to take turns, but in the first half of the century it still went on for 24 hours a day, lasted six days, and each team had to have one rider on the track at all times. Riders were still expected to be on the track for many hours. During quiet periods around 5 or 6am they would be casually circling the track, wearing warm clothes (the heating was turned off when most punters left) and steering the bike with one foot while reading the paper or eating some food. Over time promoters realised it was a pointless tradition, with hardly anyone watching at 4am anyway. By the 1960s the 24-hour routine had been replaced by evening sessions – but these were still long, dangerous and gruelling races lasting well into the early mornings.

Six-day racing was, and remains, extremely popular in places like Ghent, Munich, Berlin, Bremen, Rotterdam and other European cities through the winter months. Cut off from the outside world in an atmosphere of tobacco smoke, the smell of fried food and the din of loud rock and cheesy disco music, it's a unique atmosphere – part sport, part festival – with beer-guzzling spectators and hard-grafting athletes.

Hugh Porter rode over 20 six-days during his career, with a third of those coming in a single winter. He spoke to Chris Sidwells in the course of the research for Sidwells' book *The Long Race to Glory*:

66 The big killers were the long Madisons. They have one-hour Madisons in the six-days now, with maybe a shorter one earlier in the evening, but when I did

them, 100-kilometre Madisons were common, and
you might get three Madisons in one evening in some
sixes. It was a hard life but we had fun doing it. There
were some characters on the six-day circuit back then,
and I remember fights and some pretty good after-race
parties. 🙴

The six-day programme varies from track to track, but the
bulk of racing comprises energy-sapping Madison relay races
where two-man teams sling each other in and out of the fray
like tag wrestlers, at 30mph or more. These are interspersed
with other races, like motor-paced races and sprints, but the
core of a six-day is the Madison. The race usually lasts for
about 40 minutes, with the objective being to gain laps over
opponents – making it a race of speed and endurance.

The resting rider stays above the line halfway up the
track and rolls around getting some respite. The rider below
propels his partner back into the race using a hand-sling.
The most effective Madison team is the one that pairs a
sprinter with someone who has longer staying power – a
'stayer'. But the sprinter needs a fair amount of staying
power, and the stayer needs to be quite fast. Both Wiggins
and Clarke had a surge of speed at the end of races, which
won sprint finishes.

Doyle partnered with Wiggins in the 1983/84 and 1984/85
seasons, winning the European Madison championship in
1984, regarded as the *de facto* world title, and the prestigious
Six Days of Bremen in 1985. But Wiggins was a drinker and

party man, who soon slipped down the rankings. Doyle went on to form a partnership with Clark – they were for a while the best in the business.

As his international success grew, Doyle told his biographer Nicholson, he still trained regularly at Herne Hill. In 1981, before the world championships in Brno, Czechoslovakia, he was being paced as usual:

> " I was going very fast, probably 40mph, and virtually touching the mudguard in front of me, when the Derny misfired. I was too close to go round it, and as it coughed and spluttered I came down, sliding along on my backside for 25–30 yards. I completely skinned it. "

When Doyle was at the height of his career in 1982, he appeared at Herne Hill as the world professional pursuit champion, against Hans-Henrik Ørsted (who went on to win three gold medals, two silver and two bronze at the world championships himself) – which he won.

Although an amateur, Steve Cave was racing against the top riders at this time. He recalls Doyle and Glen Mitchell as the two big guys at the track in those days. They would slip the GLC park-keeper a few bottles of beer before taking their own motorbike on the track for a pacing session! 'They would go everywhere together and win all the Madisons,' says Cave.

Doyle was world champion again in 1986, but by that time Herne Hill's finances were so depleted that the promoters couldn't even afford to invite him and sponsorship was not forthcoming.

❋

The Inner London Education Authority was abolished in 1990 and, as with the GLC itself, which had been dissolved in 1986, its powers and assets were devolved to the London boroughs. The velodrome was transferred to the Borough of Southwark, but they really didn't know how to manage Herne Hill, alongside a large and diverse portfolio of assets including parks, cemeteries and swimming pools, so they outsourced the running to Fusion, a leisure facilities management firm.

Meanwhile, the Saffron Lane track in Leicester had been modernised with the addition of a wooden board surface in the late 1980s, and by 1990 only this track and Meadowbank in Edinburgh came anywhere near international standards in the UK. The advent of the 250-metre UCI standard for international competition in 1990 meant there was no going back for a 450-metre outdoor track like Herne Hill.

'Everything we did was for the track,' says Steve Cave. 'Road or circuits – it all came back to the track in the summer.' But everything was changing: international track racing had now become an indoor winter sport played out on regulation 250-metre tracks.

# 9

## Phoenix rising

The year 1992 was a turning point for British cycling – and Herne Hill in particular.

When Chris Boardman spectacularly caught Jens Lehmann in the 4,000-metres individual pursuit final at the Barcelona Olympics in July 1992, he was the first British cyclist to win a gold medal since Harry Ryan and Thomas Lance won the tandem sprint in 1920. In fact, since the 1948 London Games, Britain had only won four bronze medals – all in the team pursuit. The 1960s and 1980s had both been completely barren decades for British track cyclists at the Olympics.

The first British cycling gold in 72 years reignited a passion for cycling that had not been seen since the post-war years and has steadily increased ever since. It marked the beginning of Britain's renaissance as a leading nation in international cycling. Boardman's success propelled the Wirral-born rider into a professional career on the Continent, but also propelled his coach Peter Keen and, ultimately, the whole of

British cycling into a new era. In 1997 Keen was appointed by the British Cycling Federation as performance director, to devise the World Class Performance Plan, which received millions in Lottery funding and transformed the fortunes of British cycling – not just track, but eventually road racing too.

Herne Hill's fortunes were reignited in 1992 as well, when the track was rebuilt. The surface was visibly near the end of its life and a year earlier, on the 100th anniversary of its being built, Southwark Council had announced ambitious regeneration plans, to be funded by Southwark and the Sports Council, including demolishing the track and building a new one, rebuilding the grandstand, building changing rooms, improving drainage, installing a public address system and erecting floodlighting.

Design and construction of the new track was handled by Ron Webb, the leading track builder. Originally from Sydney, he was a keen cyclist in his youth, eventually becoming national champion before moving to Amsterdam in 1954 to try his luck racing in Europe where he enjoyed success in Madison and motor-paced events. On retirement he got involved in race organisation, promoting the Skol 6 series at Wembley from 1968 to 1980. His racing and management experience eventually led him into designing and building tracks.

In south London Webb discovered an eccentric track. This was not unusual in older tracks (Brighton's Preston Park, for example, was built in 1887 with four straights of unequal length; a single lap being 579 metres!), but was not what would be expected from an Olympic velodrome. The north curve was banked at 9 degrees and the south curve was 12 degrees, one curve was longer than the other, resulting in the straights also being different lengths, and the home straight had a slight incline.

Webb's new, narrower geometry brought the track circumference to 450 metres on the racing line, with steeper banking at 26 degrees and smooth transitions into each straight. The quick-drying white epoxy-resin skin on the surface was considered the fastest material at the time. There was also a new wooden safety fence, topped off with a steel rail.

Plans to rebuild the grandstand and other amenities, and add lighting around the perimeter to allow evening use in winter, failed to materialise in the face of spiralling costs and disputed funding commitments. The side stands were shut and the dozen or so club sheds underneath the stands were bricked up.

But this was still a massive improvement for Herne Hill. And it came at a time when both the Harlow and Paddington tracks had closed down, leaving Herne Hill as the only racing track in the London area. Paddington had closed in 1987 after 99 years' activity: spectators and participants had been in steady decline for two decades and the track was in such a poor state that riding stopped altogether and it was eventually demolished and grassed over. The Harlow track, by contrast, had been a fleeting bright spot in track cycle racing in this period. The tiny 180-metre timber-framed outdoor track was built in 1976 on a shoestring, with an active programme of promotions and even televised meetings in the 1980s. Steve Cave recalled that although it was a fantastic track to race on, it was built without foundations, which brought problems. 'In Madison races you'd sling your partner in and you could feel it moving,' he says. 'When you've got twelve guys hitting the same banking, you'd shit yourself. But then later you'd see some of the younger kids riding around the advertising hoardings at the top!' Unfortunately the site was abruptly sold for redevelopment in 1990 and the proceeds disappeared overseas, rather than being redeployed as promised on the UK's first indoor velodrome nearby.

The Herne Hill track rebuild, meanwhile, was completed in August 1992. Although it was still not ready for public use, after a training session in October, Dave Le Grys, who was the national sprint coach by this time, declared it 'excellent, so fast and easy to ride … It is so different to the old track where you had to look out for potholes and almost came to a standstill when you came out of the banking.'

And 1992 was also the year that the twelve-year-old Bradley Wiggins began racing at the velodrome. Wiggins was born in 1980 in Ghent, where his father Gary was based while competing in circuit races and six-day events. His parents split up when he was two and he moved to Kilburn in north-west London with his mother, to live with her parents. He grew up without contact with his father, but followed him into cycling after witnessing Boardman's heroics in Barcelona on TV and shelving his childhood plans to become a goalkeeper.

'I remember going there [to Herne Hill] as a kid with my

mum and admiring the world champions who used to be invited in their rainbow jerseys,' he told the *Guardian*, 'the sprinter Michael Hubner, the six-day racer Danny Clark and the pursuiter Tony Doyle. I used to look up to those guys and hope that one day I would be doing what they were doing.'

He trained and raced regularly at Herne Hill from 1992 onwards. He was a quietly confident lad, who generally kept himself to himself, preferring to sit in the stands listening to his Walkman between races, rather than socialising. 'I have such fond memories of Herne Hill, which played an important role in my development as a rider,' he said. 'I remember the buzz I got from racing there when I was younger and that really gave me the bug for the sport. It's such an iconic facility not just for the local area but for the whole British cycling scene.'

The first open event at the rebuilt track was scheduled to be the 1993 Good Friday Meeting featuring sprinters Michael Hubner, the world professional champion, facing fellow German Jens Friedler, the world amateur champion. It would be one of the last ever appearances of separate world amateur and professional sprint champions: shortly afterwards the UCI discontinued the distinction between the two classes, unifying both titles in a single race. George Lacy Hillier, self-appointed guardian of amateurism, would have spun in his grave.

Rain was falling on the day of the Good Friday Meeting and while the patient crowd waited to see if it would ease off and allow some racing, Hubner talked with spectators in the grandstand and entertained them by arm-wrestling with Friedler. When it was obvious no racing was going to take place, they both agreed with Graham Bristow, the promoter, to come back in late May.

When they reconvened on 29 May they produced some fantastic racing. Hubner beat Friedler by half a wheel in the sprint, but later gifted the keirin (a sprint race behind a motor pacer) to Friedler. After several years' absence, ex-world champion Tony Doyle had a hat-trick of victories in the Devil, 10-lap points and Golden Wheel (a 22-kilometre scratch race).

The programme had changed because many riders couldn't make the second date, which left some holes in the schedule. Graeme Obree asked Bristow for a slot and produced what was to be the highlight of the day, if not the decade, at Herne Hill.

Obree, the maverick genius Scot, was preparing for an attack on Francesco Moser's nine-year-old, seemingly unbreakable world hour record. Obree realised that going for Moser's hour record on an indoor track would be expensive, since there were still no indoor tracks in the UK. So he decided to break his own current British record to help find sponsorship to fund a trip overseas. Characteristically his manager, Vic Haines, told the press that Obree's target was not just his 46-kilometre British record, but ultimately Moser's 51.151-kilometre record. 'The cheek of the man,' wrote *Cycling Weekly*.

The hour is one of cycling's simplest and most brutal challenges: see how far you can get in 60 minutes. The record has been broken by some of cycling's most legendary figures, including Fausto Coppi, Jacques Anquetil and Eddy Merckx. To hold it is on a par with winning a Grand Tour, one-day Classic or world championship. But it's not good enough 'just' to be the best on the day – the ride has be the best ever. There's also no runner-up – you simply succeed or fail.

The hour is one of the oldest targets in cycling. The first record attempt is attributed to Henri Desrange at the Buffalo track in Paris in 1893, although there were attempts before that – including by the ubiquitous James Moore. Desrange rode 35.325 kilometres. The record was broken ten times before the First World War, again several times in the 1930s and then again in the 1950s, primarily at the Velodromo Vignorelli in Milan. In 1968, when the Dane Ole Ritter had the idea of exploiting the thin air of Mexico City, he managed 48.653 kilometres. Eddy Merckx went better in 1972, but it was not until 1984 that Francesco Moser broke through the 50-kilometre barrier.

Whereas Merckx had ridden a conventional bike, Moser was the first to ride an example of what became increasingly unusual, if highly effective, aerodynamic machines. He used disc wheels (which reduced the drag caused by traditional spoked wheels by 50 per cent) and they were of uneven sizes (being 7cm bigger at the back), resulting in a high seat and curiously curved, sloping top tube.

Obree famously built his own bikes from washing machine parts and rode with his handlebars under his chest and his arms tucked up beside him like a downhill skier, or praying mantis. He questioned everything and assumed nothing, preferring to trust his instinct – a man in the spirit of Alf Engers before him. He reasoned that if the bearings in a washing machine could sustain spinning at 1200rpm they would be of sufficient quality for his bike. He thought it felt more natural to spin his legs closer together than was normally the case on bikes, so he made a narrower bottom bracket and did away with the top tube, so that his knees didn't hit the frame. He called his bike 'Old Faithful': it looked uncomfortable and awkward, and was initially wobbly, but when he got up to speed he was incredibly fast.

Bristow scheduled Obree's attempt for the hour record just before the 20-kilometre race. For many spectators it was their first encounter with Obree, Old Faithful and his unconventional riding position. The crowd was quiet as he rolled away and Bristow initially thought he'd made a mistake as people started to drift off.

But as Obree built momentum and settled into his stride, the crowd started to realise they were watching something special. The announcer, Roger Shayes, gave a very knowledgeable commentary as he relayed Obree's split-times to the record. As the crowd became aware they were watching an exceptional performance, they gave him plenty of encouragement. Suddenly everyone was sucked back in, for the full hour.

Obree beat his own 10-kilometre record by 46 seconds and his 20-kilometre record by over a minute and a half. The pitch of the announcer's voice began to get more and more excited. At halfway, Obree was behind Moser's world record but he was maintaining a similar speed to Merckx's distance. A rising breeze pushed against him every time he entered the back straight, but he visibly accelerated into the home straight as the wind got behind him each time. Even the spitting rain couldn't put him off, and with a strong finish he got a new British record of 49.383 kilometres – almost 3 kilometres further than his previous best and only 50 metres short of Merckx's record which had been set at altitude in Mexico City.

The ride gave a seal of approval to the track and proved a decisive step in a career that would twice see Obree break the world hour record and win two world championships. But it was Obree's rivalry with Boardman that most captured the public imagination, as the pair battled on the international stage, alternating individual world championship victories – Obree winning in 1993 and 1995, Boardman in 1994 and 1996 – and fought for the hour record.

Boardman and Obree were very different characters, who took very different routes in life and sport. Obree's plan for the hour was straightforward – train as hard as he could, hire a velodrome and then ride as hard as he could for 60 minutes. He relied on willpower, which he had in abundance and an incredible capacity for enduring pain. Boardman was all about science, planning and predictability. It was a classic rivalry and the press played on their stereotypes: human vs robot, artist vs scientist, loner vs committee man, weirdo vs square.

'Looking back, Peter and I were nowhere near as rigorous, scientifically, as we thought we were being at the time,' remembered Boardman in an interview with Ellis Bacon:

" But Graeme's approach was just annoying. We were fascinated by the process of getting better. But Graeme came from left field – that is, he powered himself with marmalade sandwiches, and made his bike out of old bits himself, and it seemed to just be taking the piss a bit when we'd fought and worked so hard to get to the point we were at. "

In characteristic style Boardman had announced at the end of 1992 that he was slowly and methodically working towards an attempt on the hour in summer 1993. He and Keen believed the hour was an assailable target based on Boardman's performance data and worked meticulously towards an attempt in Bordeaux. Friday 23 July was a rest day towards the end of the Tour de France, the assembled cycling journalists would be looking for stories after a sprint finish in Bordeaux – so Boardman could steal the limelight of the world's press.

But in equally characteristic style, Obree had impulsively decided that he would take Moser's record from under Boardman's nose, less than two months after taking the British hour record at Herne Hill. He even tried to book Bordeaux velodrome a few weeks before Boardman, but in the end was unable to do so and opted for a track in Norway.

Obree actually failed by nearly a kilometre in his initial attempt on 16 July, but he had booked the velodrome in Hamar for 24 hours and decided to come back at 8 o'clock the next morning to try again – this time breaking Moser's record by 445 metres.

To stop his aching body seizing up overnight, Obree realised he needed to stretch his muscles regularly. He didn't want to set an alarm and shock his system abruptly, reasoning that it would be better to wake naturally. So he took the unusual step of drinking pints of water so that he woke up to go to the toilet every couple of hours through the night. Each time he got up, he stretched his muscles.

Obree's triumph lasted less than a week. On 23 July, Boardman broke his new record by 674 metres, riding 52.270 kilometres at Bordeaux. His bike had a carbon frame, carbon wheels and a triathlon handlebar.

In one week, British track cycling had grabbed the headlines. Their rivalry grew: a few months later Obree knocked Boardman out of the world championship pursuit to take the title himself. (The tables had turned, on the world stage, and both men felt awkward: after defeating Boardman in the semi, Obree reportedly said, 'Sorry about that.'). His appearance in world champion stripes in the 1994 Good Friday Meeting attracted the best crowd at Herne Hill for years.

Riding in an eight-station ten-minute Roadman's Pursuit, Obree nearly came unstuck when Nick Gritton, a local amateur rider on the station behind him, made a very fast start and almost caught him before he had got into his rhythm

– meaning he would have been eliminated. When the ten minutes had elapsed only Obree, Rob Hayles and Chris Ball were left racing. Obree ran out the winner, with Hayles second. Obree was well placed in other races, but never looked as comfortable or dazzling in bunch races.

Obree was nonetheless on fire and less than a month later he stole the hour record back in Bordeaux. But the UCI grew concerned that changes to bicycles were making a disproportionate improvement to track records. Among other measures in May 1994, it banned his riding position: he did not find out until one hour before he began the world championship pursuit in Italy. Judges disqualified him when he refused to comply.

The bottom line was that the establishment didn't like Obree and he didn't like them. When the UCI banned his tucked position, he went to the opposite extreme, inventing the 'Superman' position – using extended tri-bars with his arms fully extended in front of him so that he was stretched out even further.

Boardman later confessed to Ellis Bacon:

    &#10077; We looked at the 'Superman position' in particular, just as a nod to being open-minded. We didn't even do any measurements, like we normally would, but it took only a couple of laps of the track in that position before I went 'Oh shit. We're going to have to do this, aren't we?' The improvement was just enormous – absolutely enormous. &#10078;

The UCI banned that position too, but not before Obree had used it in winning the individual pursuit at the world championships in 1995 and Boardman had used it to break the hour record yet again in 1996.

Obree and Hayles met again in the Campagnola Pursuit at Good Friday in 1995, when they eliminated all other riders, but with two and a half minutes still remaining Hayles caught Obree and reversed the previous year's result. Hayles also won the Golden Wheel, Devil and points races. The affable, brown-haired Hayles was still only 22 years old at the time, but he would mature into a highly successful rider, accumulating thirteen track medals at Olympic, world and Commonwealth level.

Hayles also won the Campagnola Pursuit in 1996 and 1997, on the latter occasion beating into second place Sean Yates, who had just retired from Continental road racing. Yates had won the event eighteen years previously. Having competed in twelve Grand Tours, winning stages in two, the Herne Hill regular Yates was still a very popular attraction.

At the same time as the elite racing, though, there was plenty of amateur and youth racing. A meeting in June 1997 promoted by Wally Happy, who was still closely linked to the velodrome nearly 50 years after first racing there (and indeed he is still a regular visitor), included £100 first prize for the 25 miles scratch. The under-12s omnium featured Geraint Thomas for Maindy Flyers from Cardiff and Ben Swift from Ashfield Road Club in Nottinghamshire, both beaten by a local young VCL rider, Jason Cattermole.

'Travelling to race at Herne Hill, a classic cycling venue but also home to old rivals of ours, was like going to an away ground in the Six Nations,' remembered Thomas in his autobiography, 'a warm welcome, but also a sense of: this is our territory, we'll make it hard for you.'

❀

In the early 1980s cycling wasn't noticeably different to the way it had been immediately after the war – slightly faster and showier, but the same essential philosophy and beliefs. The early 1990s witnessed the start of a cataclysmic process of modernisation. New materials such as carbon-fibre made bikes lighter. Scientific training methods made riders faster. The sport opened into new markets. The line between amateur and professional was erased in 1993.

Science was taking over. The hour record was indicative of the magnitude of the shift: in the twelve years between 1984 and 1996, the record jumped from 50.808 kilometres to 56.375, a similar improvement to the 59 years between 1913 and 1972. (The alternative perspective, expressed by many riders who were racing in the 1970s and 1980s, was to lament the fact that there was much less 'rough and tumble' by the 1990s – racing had become more sanitised.)

Peter Keen became British Cycling's national coach in 1992, aged only 28. In his autobiography, *Easy Rider*, Rob Hayles wrote:

❝ The British cycling revolution owes as much to Keen

as it does to the influx of National Lottery money that was to come in a few years later. Keen completely revolutionised the way things were done. He based everything he did on evidence. There was no guess-work. He didn't go on hunches or superstition. He had no time for the phrase: 'But that's how we've always done it.' … If science didn't prove something, he disregarded it until there was some research to prove the case. 🙶

In the early 1990s Manchester (which was considering bidding for the 2000 Olympics), committed to a new indoor velodrome, also designed by Ron Webb. It opened in September 1994 and became home to the British Cycling Federation, establishing itself as the premier track in the UK, hosting the UCI Track Cycling World Championships in 1996, 2000 and 2008, as well as the 2002 Commonwealth Games.

The 1996 Olympics in Atlanta were the first Games open to professional cyclists, but they were a let-down for the British team, with a single gold from Steve Redgrave and Matthew Pinsent in the rowing (the lowest tally of golds since 1952). There wasn't a single medal in track racing and just two bronze on the road (Max Sciandri, a rider from Derby of Italian descent, and Chris Boardman). The response was the formation of UK Sport in early 1997, followed by a flood of National Lottery money into Olympic sports.

The Sports Council was now able to offer grants of up to £28,000 p.a. to elite competitors, which meant that selected athletes could concentrate on training and competing in international events, receiving the most advanced training with all their living expenses paid. The British Cycling Federation embraced the programme enthusiastically. The budget for cycling was tripled and Keen was appointed director of the new World Class Performance Plan.

All the foundations were in place for success: the money, the facility and the man with the vision.

The British Cycling Federation chose to spend Lottery funding on the 'controllable' elements of cycling, providing the best coaching and equipment. Keen focused on track cycling and women's racing, to the chagrin of the road racing fraternity. He believed medals could be won in these areas in the short term, attracting more funding and creating a virtuous cycle. But for many people, road racing was the be-all and end-all of cycling – the highest potential rewards, media attention and British Cycling Federation resources. But it was dominated by continental Europe, and other than a few outstanding individuals who had bucked the trend over the years – Tom Simpson, Robert Millar and Sean Yates, to name a few – British success had been limited. It also had a deeply ingrained culture of doping, which raised a whole raft of other issues in the context of public funding, never mind the ethics.

There were also more Olympic and world championship medals to be won on the track than the road (four Olympic road medals compared with eight for the track in 1996 and then twelve track medals from 2000), and there was less depth of competition – in simple terms, 20 people start a track race and 200 start the Tour de France – let alone the unpredictable impact of tactics and chance in a multi-day stage race.

Although things were changing for the better at a national level, it was having an effect on grass-roots cycling. 'When Manchester opened,' says Graham Bristow, 'it sucked the life-blood out of a lot of outdoor tracks, because it was a different dimension.' He believes the whole scene became Manchester-centric as British Cycling got stronger and stronger. While foreign stars still raced at Herne Hill, ironically, leading British riders based in Manchester would often be forbidden to ride elsewhere, with the coaches preferring to keep them under close supervision in the north-west.

Fundamentally, Bristow also feels that Herne Hill never really recovered from the effects of re-profiling in 1992. The track needed rebuilding because it was damaged, but it was closed for two years, and people got out of the habit of going. And when they did start again, it was a lesser experience, often with poor visibility for spectators.

When they re-profiled the track, besides increasing the steepness of the banking, the distance between the straights was reduced, making the laps slightly shorter. This had the significant effect of moving the home straight away from the grandstand. Crowds used to watch from the vantage of the grandstand and that was fine when the home straight was flat. Now there was a camber and it was further away. Spectators in the grandstand found themselves 30 feet from the action and separated from it by a crowd of people standing in front of them. The new track also made the shabbiness of the rest of the infrastructure even more obvious.

The impact on racing was compounded by the fact that promoters also stopped charging spectators – other than for Good Friday and the Champagne Meeting – in the late 1980s/ early 1990s, preferring to encourage greater attendance and seek revenue via sponsorship. Again race promoter Graham Bristow feels this was a mistake that was to have long-term ramifications for race meetings at the track:

> " I never subscribed to not paying for entry. All the meetings were funded by spectators. You need to put on a show, provide the entertainment and spectators will come to watch it. Then you have money for prizes and the riders' expenses. They were the actors. "

There wasn't a profit motive behind the race meetings, at least not in the 1970s and 1980s, but there was a sustainable model to keep the race scene going. Spectators and competitors paid money, which went back into upkeep and riders' prizes. As the revenues declined, so did the ability to bring in big names, and big names bring big crowds. It became a vicious circle. Bristow goes on:

> " I take the view that if something doesn't have a price tag on it, then it has little or no value. Others

disagreed and said that there should be free admission to spectators to encourage them to come. As a promoter I would rather have 1,000 paying spectators than 2,000 non-paying. 🙶

Spectators at meetings like Good Friday fell towards 2,000–3,000 in the 1990s, but despite the changed scale of competition there was a regular programme of races on Monday and Wednesday evenings, and many Saturday afternoons. Training and coaching sessions for all ages and abilities were organised and run by Dave Creasey and Russell Williams (who now also coached) and a 1¼-mile mountain bike/cyclo-cross circuit built on waste ground behind the track was in regular use throughout the year.

So although there weren't many spectators, lots of people were using the track – or rather the 'velodrome'. It was around this time that Southwark started promoting the facility as Herne Hill Velodrome, rather than a stadium.

It was also around this time that Bradley Wiggins began to emerge as the world-beater he would become. In 1999, a pursuit race between Wiggins – who in seven short years had emerged as world junior pursuit champion – and Ian Hallam, world masters pursuit champion, was billed as a match of youth against age and experience. Wiggins won, and went on to win the Campagnola Pursuit for the next two years.

By the turn of the century the World Class Performance Plan was starting to bear fruit. At the Good Friday Meeting in 2000 the British national sprint team of Jason Queally, Chris

Hoy and Craig MacLean avenged their defeat in the final of the world championship in Berlin the previous October by beating the French team of Laurent Gané, Florian Rousseau and Arnaud Tournant.

The Sydney Olympics in 2000 marked another landmark in the journey of British cycling, with the track cycling team contributing a gold, silver and two bronze medals – justifying even more Lottery cash. The men's sprint trio were pushed back into silver medal position as the French team reasserted their dominance. In the men's team pursuit Bryan Steel, Paul Manning, Bradley Wiggins and Chris Newton avenged this defeat by beating the French team for bronze.

Yvonne McGregor also won bronze in the women's individual pursuit, becoming the first ever female British track cycling Olympic medallist. She was 39 at the time and had competed in running until the age of 28. She started cycling competitively when she took up triathlon and then focused on it after an Achilles injury. In 1993 she broke Beryl Burton's 20-year-old British 10-mile time trial record, won a gold medal in the points race at the 1994 Commonwealth Games in Canada, set an hour record for women in June 1995 and broke Burton's 25-mile time trial record in 1996. Less than two months after winning gold in Sydney, she won the women's individual pursuit gold at the 2000 world championships in Manchester.

But it was Jason Queally's gold medal in the 1-kilometre time trial ('the kilo') – and the fact that he broke the Olympic record in the process – that reinforced the progress British cycling was making. Queally had nearly died in an accident at Meadowbank track in Edinburgh when an 18-inch sliver of the wooden track entered his chest via his armpit. The accident seriously affected his confidence in bunch racing, so he subsequently focused on the kilo, team sprint and time trial events. In addition to his two Olympic medals in Sydney he won eight world championship medals in his career.

By this time the British Cycling Federation had also rebranded itself as British Cycling, and helped unify the sport, absorbing most other bodies representing the various branches of cycling. Dave Brailsford also got more heavily involved and Shane Sutton took over as the sprint team manager in 2002. Having joined as an adviser when Lottery funding began in 1997, Brailsford became programme director, working with Keen before taking over as performance director in 2003 when Keen moved on. He built on Keen's remarkable success, but took things to new heights with his concept of 'marginal gains'. 'The whole principle came from the idea that if you broke down everything you could think of that goes into riding a bike, and then improved it by 1 per cent,' he later told the BBC, after his strategy had borne fruit in the London Olympics, 'you will get a significant increase when you put them all together.'

Through the second half of the 1990s a sword hung over the fate of Herne Hill track yet again. Cycle sport was still in the doldrums – the renaissance being very much a work in progress at this time (even the new Manchester Velodrome was poorly used) – and Southwark was under pressure to justify the ongoing funding. The council had only carried out minimal repairs to the general facilities for a number of years, apart from the work done to the track in 1992. Typically there would be a site visit at the start of each year, followed by essential repairs to get the grounds into reasonable shape for Easter and hopefully the season. The grandstand was rotten to the core and covered in a patchwork of hardboard repairs.

The 42-year 'full-repairing lease' was due to expire in March 2002. It was a dire situation. Southwark lacked the resources, rationale or enthusiasm for funding and managing a facility that wasn't particularly well-used, in the face of tight budgets and many other deserving commitments. Yet they were reluctant to end the lease, because they would become liable to the landowners, the Dulwich Estate, for a substantial sum for dilapidation over their period as leasee. And Sport England would also be able to claim back money they had provided for rebuilding the track.

There seemed no solution, but at least the Dulwich Estate allowed the ongoing use of the track on the understanding that Southwark would be responsible for the site, even if they didn't renew the lease. An eighteen-month lease was agreed in summer 2002, allowing temporary reprieve and some degree of certainty that the centenary Good Friday Meeting could go ahead in 2003.

It turned out to be a glorious celebration of 100 years' history, with a star-studded international field, fine weather and over 5,000 paying spectators: the largest crowd in years.

Huge interest was generated by the announcement that three Tour de France stage winners would face Bradley Wiggins in an all-star ten-minute Roadman's Pursuit. The Malta-born Scottish rider David Millar had enjoyed significant success on the road, with stage wins in the Tour and Vuelta. He was joined by two Australians: Stuart O'Grady, who had won two stages in the Tour, and would go on to win gold in the men's madison at the 2004 Olympics and Paris–Roubaix in 2007; plus Brad McGee, the reigning world pursuit champion, who would go on to win gold and silver at the following year's Olympics.

Local boy Wiggins by this stage had built on his world junior pursuit championship win in 1998 and Olympic bronze for team pursuit in 2000 to show his huge potential going forward. Indeed, he would go on to win the world individual pursuit title in August.

Another Australian, Sean Eadie, the world sprint and keirin champion, was also due to race against Scottish stars Ross Edgar and Chris Hoy. The six-foot, 98kg Eadie was known for his bushy black beard, and an aggressive style at odds with his off-track gentleness (he was a primary school teacher before turning professional). Hoy was at this stage the reigning world kilo and team sprint champion, whereas Edgar, Hoy's teammate in the Commonwealth bronze-winning team pursuit, had beaten an illustrious international field to win the sprint and the highly coveted *News of the World* Trophy at the previous year's Good Friday Meeting.

Although Millar and Eadie both dropped out due to injuries, it was still a great success in great weather – and Millar was in attendance even though he didn't ride, sporting visible injuries from his fall in the Paris–Nice race.

The final sprint for the Champion of Champions trophy was between Italian Roberto Chiappa, the winner in 2001, and Hoy wearing the coveted rainbow jersey – with the British Olympian winning by half a wheel. There was a landmark victory for Denise Hampson, the former British women's sprint champion who competed for Team GB more than twenty times, when she qualified through the heats to beat Ross Edgar and other top sprinters in the 500-metre handicap. This was the first Good Friday win by a woman since the introduction of mixed racing in 1987.

The highlight of the afternoon, though, was the ten-minute pursuit race with McGee, O'Grady, Wiggins and Paul Manning – another member of the medal-winning GB pursuit team. The riders were evenly matched, with Manning having a slight advantage by halfway, but then Wiggins upped his pace a fraction and with perfectly judged effort steadily drew level with Manning to finish 14 metres ahead. McGee was third and O'Grady fourth.

The other big event was the 20-kilometre Golden Wheel scratch race. World points champion Chris Newton broke away after only three laps and opened a sizeable gap against a field also including Sean Yates. O'Grady with three others joined Newton and, working together, they gained half a lap on the bunch. With a dozen laps to go, Wiggins took up the chase and dragged ten riders relentlessly towards the breakaways. But Newton went off the front again with five laps remaining, and as the bell went for the last lap it looked as though he was safe, but Wiggins led the remnants of the field past him on the final banking. Tony Gibb made an all-out sprint for the line, but O'Grady worked his wheel until the last moment and won by inches.

The centenary Good Friday Meeting was a huge success, but it wasn't held the following year because it clashed with the world championships in Manchester – and it never really picked up again after that. The south London track itself was now very much in the shadow of the shiny rival in Manchester, but it was forging a new role as it rode the wave of cycling's new-found popularity.

# Herne Hill is the place I love

Prior to 2004 Britain had a reputation for producing brilliant world-class riders every couple of generations. Reg Harris in the 1940s and 1950s; Tom Simpson, Barry Hoban and Hugh Porter in the 1960s and 1970s; Tony Doyle in the 1980s and Chris Boardman and Graeme Obree in the 1990s. But they were not products of the system – they succeeded despite the system.

Boardman's Olympic gold medal in 1992 had been a watershed, but it was another eight years before the next – achieved by Jason Queally in Sydney. By the Athens Olympics in 2004, British Cycling's World Class Performance Plan was bearing fruit in abundance. Britain won four medals, of which two were gold: Chris Hoy in the kilo and Bradley Wiggins in the individual pursuit. They also won silver in the team pursuit (Steve Cummings, Rob Hayles, Paul Manning and Wiggins) and bronze in the Madison (Rob Hayles and Wiggins again). So three medals for the youth who learned his race craft at Herne Hill.

But there was limited impact at Herne Hill in these early days of modern British cycling success. Graham Bristow is sceptical about the legacy:

> It's great that we're winning medals as a nation, but it's almost like there are two sports. People are being brought onto the programme, but as soon as they miss the numbers they're kicked out. But they don't go back to the clubs, they're just lost to the sport. I don't think it's really helping the grass-roots sport.

Worse still, when the national celebrations had subsided, the short-term lease for Herne Hill came to an end. Southwark weren't maintaining the facility to an acceptable level, on the assumption they were about to be kicked out. One night a bunch of riders broke in like vigilantes to jet-wash the track and fix the grandstand floor with sheets of plywood. But after four or five years' discussion, landowners the Dulwich Estate were losing faith in plans ever coming to fruition. There was a massive hole in funding for disproportionately ambitious plans – which at one stage had involved world-renowned, avant-garde Spanish architect Santiago Calatrava presenting designs for a three-storey building with climbing wall, neo-futuristic grandstand with arced lighting overhanging the home straight, and a part-covered track.

Eventually the Dulwich Estate lost patience and on 1 January 2005 the stadium was shut, without any sign of long-term agreement between them and Southwark Council, although Bristow persuaded the Dulwich Estate to at least allow the Good Friday Meeting to go ahead. They opened the grounds a week before Easter to allow a team of volunteers enough time to pull up the weeds and then locked the gates again on Easter Monday.

In late spring Peter King who ran British Cycling met with John Major (namesake of the former prime minister) who ran the Dulwich Estate; they were both accountants by training and spoke the same language. King got a favourable response when he asked about the feasibility of reopening the velodrome if British Cycling took on a short-term lease. An interim three-year lease was agreed in July so at least cycling could carry on while negotiations continued. But British Cycling needed someone to run it – and they looked towards VC Londres, which by this time was being run by Peter Cattermole, who had a strong business background. VCL agreed to work in partnership with British Cycling and the surrounding cycling community to take responsibility for the day-to-day management of the venue on a voluntary basis for the duration of the lease.

The grandstand, built when the track had first opened its doors back in 1891, was finally closed for health and safety reasons. Herne Hill Velodrome was officially reopened on 5 August 2005 with past champions including Chris Boardman and Tony Doyle present.

Although on the surface things weren't hugely positive, the fact was that Herne Hill was reinventing itself. Cattermole, who had come back to the track as a parent in the 1990s after fifteen years' absence and witnessed the community spirit, and who now found himself running the show, shared the vision for the velodrome: run by cyclists, for cyclists of all ages and abilities became the new mantra. Racing has always been, and always will be, central to Herne Hill's identity and purpose, but in order to survive they recognised the wisdom of embracing the growing popularity of cycling.

Cattermole began to make changes in order to safeguard the future. The few remaining staff were made redundant as part of drastic cost-saving measures, but several came back and helped out on a voluntary basis – the ever-present Dave Creasey being one of them. He had to scrap the Monday night 'comp' meetings which had been a staple of the Herne Hill race programme for many years. In recent years riders had often opted for either Monday or Wednesday, so numbers for both could be poor. Scrapping the Monday meetings focused attention on Wednesday and built that into a more sustainable and popular event.

Riding through the winter of 2005/06 wasn't really possible because the track was too slippery, but the volunteers cut more paths to make a 3½-mile off-road trail, and started to run the first few cyclo-cross races at Herne Hill.

At the 2007 world championships in Palma de Mallorca, Spain, the British team won seven of the seventeen gold medals on offer. It was a watershed moment: the first time Team GB truly dominated the world. One week later, Bradley Wiggins and Victoria Pendleton rode a lap of honour at the Good Friday Meeting at Herne Hill to celebrate their achievements – Wiggins had won the individual pursuit and team pursuit in Spain, Pendleton the women's sprint, keirin and team sprint.

Wiggins was the star attraction in south London, winning both the ten-minute pursuit as well as the fifteen-lap elimination race. He pushed Academy youngster Alex Dowsett into second spot in the pursuit, with Jason Allen third. He beat Tony Gibb in the elimination race, while Allen was third once again. But in the Golden Wheel 18-kilometre scratch race Wiggins was pushed off the podium, Allen stealing the win after a late solo attack from Wiggins was caught on the final lap. Dowsett took second and Gibb third. Double world champion in sprint and team sprint, Germany's Jan van Eijden, won the invitation sprint.

Despite not riding, Victoria Pendleton received rapturous applause from the huge crowd for her achievements in Palma when she presented the prizes.

British track cycling was at its zenith in 2008. At the world championships at Manchester in March, Team GB won nine gold medals, out of a possible eighteen. 'Just unbelievable! We've crushed everybody,' said Dave Brailsford, talking to Richard Moore for Moore's book *Heroes, Villains & Velodromes*. 'I don't think there's another word for it.' One magazine described it as the best performance by any British team – ever.

Come the Beijing Olympics in August it took only moments to overcome any lingering doubts that they could repeat their performance. Brailsford said:

" As soon as the team sprint boys got up and broke the world record with their first ride, Shane Sutton and I looked at each other and went: 'Shit, we're going to get a lot of medals.' We knew, at that moment, that our calibration was right. "

Nicole Cook opened the floodgates with gold in the road race, followed by Emma Pooley taking silver in the time trial. But on the track Team GB took an incredible seven out of ten gold medals. Bradley Wiggins took gold in the individual pursuit, and the team pursuit with Paul Manning, Ed Clancy and Geraint Thomas. Rebecca Romero and Victoria Pendleton both took gold medals, in the individual pursuit and sprint respectively. Chris Hoy won three golds in the sprint, keirin and team sprint alongside Jason Kenny and Jamie Staff. Kenny, Wendy Houvenaghel and Ross Edgar also took individual silver medals, while Chris Newton and Steven Burke both collected bronze. A phenomenal haul.

Following the Olympic successes there were long queues at Herne Hill on Saturday mornings as the numbers of people wanting induction classes, coached training sessions and casual riding all increased. The range of activities was also slowly extending, with more schools visiting regularly.

Many of the Olympic heroes appeared at the following year's Good Friday Meeting: Ed Clancy, Ross Edgar and

Chris Newton were joined by former world champion and the current national road race champion Rob Hayles, with international competition coming from Spaniards Toni Tauler, who won silver in Beijing, and Carlos Torrent who won bronze in Athens.

'I've always been impressed with the huge crowds at the Herne Hill track, in particular at the Good Friday Meeting,' says Ed Clancy. 'It was always fascinating to watch Brad Wiggins, Paul Manning and Tony Gibb compete there. For me it's a great track to ride, and amazing to have one that's accessible to riders of all abilities.'

That's a culture Graham Bristow has always sought to maintain:

> " The great thing about the International Sprint at Good Friday is that it's not just the big boys fighting it out for glory – local club riders are given a chance to take on some of the best in the world and see if they can upset the apple cart. "

Although the reality is that through the years, whoever won the sprint at Good Friday would often go on to win the world championships too.

From 2008 to 2010 the Dulwich Estate had allowed the site to be used under yearly licence arrangement, with VCL managing the track on behalf of British Cycling. By 2010, however, the velodrome was threatened with closure yet again. Although the track laid in 1992 was designed to last for 20 years, it had been deteriorating steadily. While fast to ride on, it soon became slippery with algal growth and was too dangerous to use in wet weather. It was also becoming abrasive and cracking on the surface

Local residents, parents of young riders and the established cycling community at Herne Hill all joined forces. A public meeting in the Great Hall of Dulwich College in October 2010 was held to launch the Save the Velodrome campaign. The campaign generated media coverage in the mainstream and cycling press and attracted interest across the world, as well as support from local MP Tessa Jowell, Olympic legend Seb Coe, who had led the London bid for the Olympics, and Mayor of London Boris Johnson.

The Herne Hill Velodrome Trust was set up in January 2011, with responsibility for ensuring the sustainable redevelopment of the site. In early 2011 the Dulwich Estate and British Cycling reached an agreement on the lease for the track and infield that would last for fifteen years, and a three-year renewable lease on the rest of the site. This longer lease in turn unlocked an investment by British Cycling of £400,000, for phase one of the regeneration plan: resurfacing the track with a faster, all-weather tarmac surface and installing new trackside safety fencing. This was completed in autumn 2011.

While there was a very active cycling programme, the use and long-term viability of the velodrome was hampered by the lack of modern facilities and shelter. The iconic old pavilion had by this point long been derelict; the toilets were located in Portakabins and the café was a tent. The infrastructure was in desperate need of renewal, not only to cope with the surge in interest but to ensure that the site was financially sustainable for years to come. But phases two and three of the regeneration plan would have to wait until after the Olympics.

Preparations for London 2012 helped generate huge interest in Herne Hill, including the 'Going for Gold' day in early 2012, which featured Tommy Godwin, the now 92-year-old double-bronze winner of 1948, riding a lap of honour.

On 22 July 2012 crowds gathered for an open race meeting at Herne Hill, then massed around large TV screens to watch Wiggins helping teammate Mark Cavendish to his fourth consecutive victory on the Champs-Élysées and claim his own victory in the Tour de France to become the first ever British rider to win the general classification.

Two weeks later at the London Olympics Wiggins won the men's time trial on the road, with Chris Froome getting silver, while Lizzie Armitstead claimed silver in the road race.

But on the track Team GB again annihilated the opposition, winning seven out of a possible ten gold medals. Laura Trott won two gold medals: in the team pursuit with Joanna Rowsell and Danni King, and also the women's omnium. Victoria Pendleton won gold in the keirin. Geraint Thomas, Steven Burke, Ed Clancy and Peter Kennaugh took gold in the team pursuit. Jason Kenny claimed the sprint gold and Chris Hoy won the keirin; they both came together to claim gold alongside Philip Hindes in the team sprint.

This equalled the gold haul at Beijing and left Chris Hoy as the most successful British Olympian ever.

❋

While elite British cycling was enjoying global domination, there was a knock-on effect: a massive boom in participation at grass-roots level. Back in 2005 British Cycling only had 15,000 members: just prior to the 2012 London Olympics it had already grown to 42,500, but by early 2016 it had soared to 140,000 members. Cycling events across the board, including road, track, mountain bike and BMX races, had risen by more than 50 per cent since 2008. In the past fifteen years, the number of under-18s who cycle competitively has risen from fewer than 1,000 to more than 14,000. Cycling is now the third most popular participation sport after swimming and running in England, with more than 2 million adults riding bikes at least once a week (excluding commuting). Ian Drake, the chief executive of British Cycling, spoke to the *Financial Times* in 2015:

> Cycling has been the first real example where elite success in major events can be properly used to get people enthused. We set out a plan in 1997 to become the world's top cycling nation and we achieved that in 2008. But the target was expressed in gold medals when really it should be about participation and getting more people on bikes.

But the impact of international success has clearly been felt beyond competitive cycling: many more people across the country are now riding for pleasure and everyday transport. Cycle traffic has risen every year since 2008. 'In the last two years, cycling has become trendy,' said Chris Boardman back in 2010. 'Two years ago, if you rode to work you were the geeky, smelly guy. Now it's a small boast.'

Phase two of the regeneration programme, completed in 2013, was funded by Southwark's Olympic Legacy programme. It included the construction of a new 250-metre inner track to enable the development of bike skills in younger riders – and as a warm-up and cool-down track for riders in events – and also a MUGA (multi-use games area) in the track centre for activities such as riding for people with disabilities, bikeability for kids and bike polo for hipsters. Low-level perimeter lighting was also added, allowing much longer hours of use during winter months.

Phase three, the removal of the old pavilion and stands, to be replaced with new facilities and improved site layout and parking, finally got under way in early 2016, following the most welcome signing of a 99-year lease between the Dulwich Estate and British Cycling. The Velodrome Trust worked with architects and finance professionals to produce a modest scheme and sustainable business plan which was funded by The Marathon Trust, Sport England, The Mayor's Fund and Southwark Council. The plan is for a new building with a club room, café area, meeting room, changing rooms and showers.

After 125 years of action, Herne Hill Velodrome remains a sustainable, vibrant community-based centre for cycling, for cyclists of all ages and abilities. There are more people than ever training and riding on the track: from an open-air track used Easter to September it has evolved into a year-round venue. It actively encourages the participation of children and young people, working with teenagers at local secondary schools and maintaining the ever-popular school holiday clubs, but also providing strider bikes and frog bikes for younger children at primary schools and earlier. There is also Wheels for Wellbeing, a charity that helps people with disabilities to cycle using a wide variety of specially designed bikes, such as hand-bikes.

True to its heritage as the pre-eminent cycle track in the UK, Herne Hill also provides substantial training and race opportunities for competitive cyclists. The velodrome now hosts more open race meetings than any other cycle track in the country. It may no longer get the international racing that now goes to Lee Valley and Manchester, but elite riders are bred there, and they train and race there. Peter Cattermole says:

> 66 From our point of view racing at Manchester or Lee Valley is proving a point. Here we are on an outdoor track in London and yet we can still come and beat you. We didn't see ourselves and I still don't think we do see ourselves as a 'feeder' for anywhere. We are what we are, and we do what we do. 99

In addition to the open race meetings, there's the regular

Wednesday night track league throughout the summer, a new sprint league and now a veterans' league for over-40s. Meanwhile, VeloJam is an extension of the weekly women-only track racing sessions run by cycling team MuleBar Girl-Sigma Sport and is the only event in the UK where women can race against those of similar ability. 'You can either race with the boys, or you can enter women's races and be up against national level riders,' said Wiesia Kuczaj, one of the team's managers. 'There was an obvious gap and the aim of VeloJam was to bridge that gap.'

The Good Friday Meeting moved to Lee Valley VeloPark in 2014, partly to avoid the ever-present threat of the meeting being cancelled due to rain, partly to exploit the opportunity to build on the world-class facilities at the Olympic venue, to help elevate the event back to its former glory. It's still promoted by Graham Bristow, after 30-odd years. 'I used to take the whole week off work, because I was on such a high when I organised successful meetings,' he remembers. 'That's priceless, but when it rains …' he trails off. He's now working on a three-year plan to reinvigorate the status of the event. He wants to retain a strong element of open competition with good prizes, but also return to days of high-quality invitation races to rekindle the aspirational nature of the event.

The Dave Creasey 6 meeting perhaps best captures the spirit of the venue as it approaches 125 years. It was started in 2011 to celebrate the massive contribution Creasey made over the course of nearly five decades coaching at Herne Hill up until his death in 2010. He was an unpaid volunteer by that stage, and known to many as 'the man with the keys': he was at the track from first thing in the morning until last thing at night, every single day – his arrival announced by the clattering of the 50-plus keys hanging from his belt. 'He didn't do it for any reason other than he loved Herne Hill,' says John Scripps, 'and he loved the sport.'

The DC6 follows the spirit of the European six-day races that Dave loved, with loud cheesy Euro pop, cheap beer, spluttering dernys and great madison racing. In 2015 it was extended to a two-day meeting, with the Saturday night event held at the Lee Valley VeloPark and the Sunday races held at Herne Hill, showcasing both of London's iconic Olympic velodromes in one great event. It's symbolic of the successful approach to ensure the survival of Herne Hill in tandem with the new Olympic velodrome: one of cooperation rather than competition. Although as John Scripps puts it: 'Lee Valley is an amazing venue, but it's where I work. I grew up at Herne Hill – that's the place I love.'

One of the youngsters who stood up in front of 600-odd supporters at the inaugural Save the Velodrome meeting in the Great Hall at Dulwich College back in 2010, as an aspirational ten-year old, was Fred Wright. The small blond-haired boy, in blue and red VC Londres kit, told the gathered supporters and media how he dreamed of becoming a professional cyclist one day. He talked of his admiration for fellow Herne Hill alumnus Bradley Wiggins, and of his ambition to win an Olympic gold medal on the track and take part in the Grand Tours on the road.

Since then he has won six national youth titles, nine gold medals at the UK School Games and a bronze medal in the European Youth Olympics, not to mention winning Herne Hill senior track league in 2014/15 as a sixteen-year old! He was on the British Cycling Talent Team in 2013/14, the British Cycling Olympic Development Programme in 2014/15 and is now in the British Cycling Junior Academy. In other words he is a cycling talent – a product of the new system, a product of Herne Hill.

'It's hard for me to say exactly what Herne Hill means to me because it means so much,' he says.

> I first rode there when I was eight and now I'm part of British Cycling's Junior Olympic Academy. It's where I've grown up as a cyclist. If I do fulfil my dream of competing for my country and becoming a pro rider it'll be massively down to Herne Hill; all the people who've coached me there and all the people I've ridden and raced with. I owe the place everything.

# Appendix 1
# Race formats

There are countless race formats and countless variations on a theme at velodromes across the world, with the only real consistency being for the UCI-regulated events.

## Australian Pursuit

A handicap race where riders start equally spaced around the track and race for a set distance. Once a rider is caught by another rider, they are eliminated from the race. The object is to catch as many riders as possible until there are only two remaining. The winner is the first of the remaining riders to cross the line.

## Devil, Devil-Take-the-Hindmost, Elimination, Miss and Out

A race that whittles the field down by eliminating the last man in each lap (the 'hindmost') until only a few remain, at which point the bell is rung and they fight it out in the final lap.

The back of the pack at the bottom of the track is generally the worst place to be (except at the beginning of the race when the top of the track can be blocked as large numbers of stragglers try to pass over the group). After a few laps, when the field is smaller, riders surge over the top at the last minute, leaving the riders at the back stuck (the riders at the front don't need to sprint because they are safe). Some riders will play at being nearly caught out each lap, only to sprint past another rider at the last second.

### Flying Lap, Flying 200

A race from a rolling start where riders wind up their speed over several laps and then dive down the banking to hit maximum speed with 200 metres or a lap to go, to see who can cover the allotted distance in the fastest time. Traditionally used to seed racers for the sprint race.

### Italian Pursuit

A team pursuit race where each team (with any number of riders) drops a rider at the completion of every lap until only one rider per team is left to race in the final lap. The winner is the team with the fastest finish time.

### Keirin

A sprint race led by a pacer on a bike or motorcycle. The race takes two forms, the UCI event differing from the original Japanese phenomenon.

International keirin is a relatively new discipline,

having been introduced to world championships in 1980 and Olympics in 2000. Six riders line up behind a motorised derny bike, which gradually accelerates to about 50kph before it pulls off the track with around 600 metres to go, leaving a massed sprint. The first rider across the line wins. It's typically a 2-kilometre race.

Keirin racing originally began in Japan in 1948 and it remains the pre-eminent form of track cycling there – a riot of colour, power and speed. Riders wear motorcycle helmets and each wears a distinctive, vibrantly coloured top to distinguish one from the other, plus padding and knuckle gloves. Nine riders line up behind a nominated rider who paces the field, before peeling off and leaving the rest to sprint for the line.

## Kilometre Time Trial, The 'Kilo'
A race against the clock in which each rider takes to the track alone for a one-kilometre sprint, usually just over one minute of all-out effort from a standing start. There are no rounds or heats – just one chance, and the fastest time wins. The kilo is considered by many to be the most challenging track event, requiring acceleration, speed and endurance. It was removed from the Olympics after 2004.

## Longest Lap, Marymoor Crawl
A bizarre, crowd-pleasing race which originated at Marymoor Velodrome in Washington, USA in 2005. Riders set off at the beginning of the home straight and have to track-stand to ensure they do not cross the start/finish line until the bell

rings. Riders get eliminated if they put a foot down, grab the rail, ride off the track surface, fall, touch another rider or ride backwards during the track-standing period. The trick is to get as close to the line as possible for the start, but in doing so the rider risks losing balance in his attempts to avoid crossing the line early. The 'go-slow' usually lasts an unknown time, three to four minutes, until the bell rings and the sprint lap begins, with the first across the line winning.

## Madison

A massed-start endurance race, in which teams of two riders (typically a sprinter and an all-round pursuit rider) take turns racing. It features in both UCI races and also six-day race programmes, and is generally over 50 kilometres, with points every 10 or 20 laps, the first four riders across the line at each points lap winning points (five, three, two, one). The idea is to gain laps over opponents; if more than one team is on the same number of laps, the team with the greatest number of points earned in the sprints is the winner. This makes it a race of both speed and endurance.

The resting rider stays above the line halfway up the track and rolls around getting some respite while his partner races. When a man tires or finishes an agreed number of laps, the resting partner drops down and takes over the race via a 'hand-sling' into the race. As many as eighteen teams may be riding at any one time – eighteen riders competing while their partners slowly circle the top of the track; it can look very confusing for uninitiated spectators.

## Motor-paced Race

A distance race, where 'stayers' ride behind motorbikes (small dernys or 'big motors') increasing in speed up to 80kph, and offering windbreaks and streamlining. Tactics are communicated between the 'pacer' and stayer by shouts and hand signals. Races typically last for an hour or are a set distance such as 50 kilometres. There can be up to eight pacers and riders at any one time.

## Omnium

A multi-race event, which varies from programme to programme for amateurs, but for UCI events consists of six races held over two days: scratch, individual pursuit, elimination, time trial, flying lap and points race. It's best suited to an all-rounder with speed and endurance.

Points are awarded for each of the first five races, with the first rider receiving 40 points, second receiving 38, third receiving 36 and so on until 21st place. These points are added to each rider's points gained in the final points race – and the winner of the omnium is the rider with the most points in total. (Conversely, in amateur omnium the winner for each individual race gets one point, second gets two points and so forth – with the ultimate winner being the rider with the least points.)

The omnium replaced the individual pursuit, points race and madison at the Olympics in 2012.

## Points, Point-to-Point

An endurance race which encourages speed and excitement

by awarding points for intermediate sprint laps, with the winner being the rider who accumulates the most points, not necessarily the first over the line at the finish.

The first four riders across the line on predetermined sprint or points laps are awarded points (five, three, two, one). Any rider who laps the field wins 20 points. It's a very tactical event with some riders relying on endurance to gain laps while others gamble by putting all their effort into one sprint, and others spread their effort and race opportunistically.

### Pursuit (Individual)

A timed event from a standing start, where two riders begin on opposite sides of the track, and the rider with the fastest time over a given distance wins. Riders are seeded and progress through qualifying rounds to a final. As part of the omnium the distance is 3 kilometres, but otherwise it's 4 kilometres for men and 3 kilometres for women.

Trainers will stand ahead of or behind each rider's start line to indicate to the rider whether he is ahead of or behind schedule. In a final, the race stops if one rider overtakes the other. It's a test of power and judgement, with riders aiming to finish without an ounce of energy left.

### Pursuit (Team)

A timed event from a standing start, where two teams of riders begin on opposite sides of the track and the team with the fastest time over a given distance wins. Teams of four riders compete for 4 kilometres. They are seeded based on time.

The fastest eight teams progress to the next round and compete in one more round to earn their seeding for the final.

Riders begin in a row across the track. A nominated starter gets the team up to speed, forming a pace line with wheels almost touching. Each rider then takes half-lap or one-lap turns at the front, before pulling up the banking and dropping in at the end of the line. In a final, if one team overtakes the other they win, otherwise the winner is determined by the time of the third rider. Often the strongest rider will go all-out on the front towards the end, before dropping out of the race, leaving the remaining riders to cross the line in a row across the track.

## Reverse Win and Out, Belgian Win and Out

A race where the bell is rung after a designated number of neutral laps and the winner of the next lap is the fifth-place winner and retires from the race. The bell is rung again and the winner of the next lap is the fourth-place winner, and retires from the race. This continues until the bell is rung for the final time and the winner of that lap is the first-place winner.

This is a very strategic and exciting race, where riders essentially need to make a judgement call as to their best finish position – or gamble on waiting until a later round, but possibly racing against stronger riders and coming away with nothing.

## Scratch Race

These are straightforward bunch races for a set distance, with the winner being the first across the line. The current UCI distance for scratch races in the Olympic omnium and world championships is 15 kilometres, but they can be any distance.

### Snowball, Avalanche

A points race over a predetermined number of laps. The first rider across the line in the first lap is awarded one point, the first rider across the line on the second lap is awarded two points and so on. The winner is the rider who accumulates most points over the course of the race.

### Sprint (Individual)

A race between a small number of riders from a rolling or push start over a set distance, usually 1,000 metres, where the first to cross the line wins. Riders are seeded (usually by flying 200-metre times) and try to progress through elimination heats, featuring two, three or four riders, until the two fastest meet in the final, which is run as the best of three races.

Riders generally don't go all-out for the race, but employ cat-and-mouse tactics to gain an edge before the final sprint. Sprinters may bring their bikes to a standstill and feign attacks in an attempt to trick or force the other man to take the lead, or push him on to the barrier to restrict his moves. But when the jump happens, it is all-out effort to create space and prevent the opponent from benefitting from the slipstream.

### Sprint (Team)

A timed race between two teams (three riders for men, two riders for women), with the teams starting on different sides of the track. Riders line up side by side on the start line and begin from a standing start with holders, before forming a pace line going around the track. On the inside is the lead-out man, who rides the first lap flat out and then swings up the banking; the next rider leads for lap two; in the men's event the anchor man then rides the third lap, on his own, to record the team's finish time.

### Unknown Distance

A race where officials determine the length of the race in advance, but don't tell the competitors – who begin without knowing whether they will be riding one lap or 20 laps (or anywhere in between). The final lap is signalled by the bell and it's a race to be the first across the line.

### Win and Out

A race where the bell is rung after a designated number of neutral laps and the winner of the next lap wins – and pulls out. The race continues, with the first person to cross the line on the next lap also pulling out and taking second place. The race continues for a set number of laps, with the last laps generally being a sprint for the remaining places.

# Appendix 2
# Track slang and jargon

**aero**: aerodynamically efficient.

**aero bars**: forward extension of the handlebars allowing
the rider to rest his elbows and benefit from improved
aerodynamics. Only used in time trial and pursuit
races: not in bunch races where stability and control is
compromised.

**attack**: a sudden attempt to accelerate or break away from
other riders.

**back straight**: the straight part of the track, opposite the
finish line.

**banking**: a slope on the turns, allowing riders to travel
through them at speed, with the centrifugal and
gravitational forces counteracting each other to keep the
bike perpendicular to the riding surface. Banking can be
up to 50 degrees on small, indoor tracks.

**bell lap**: the last lap of a race, announced by ringing a bell.

**block**: to slow or disrupt the progress of another cyclist or breakaway.

**blow up**: to suddenly run out of energy and to be unable to continue at the required pace. *Also* bonk, hit the wall, zonk.

**blue band**: the inner edge of the track; out of bounds and no passing. Also known as Cote d'Azur.

**blue line**: a blue line in the middle of the track, for use in Madison races. Resting riders circulate above the blue line, until they are handslung back into action. *Also* stayer's line.

**bonk**: to suddenly run out of energy and be unable to continue at the required pace. *Also* blow up, hit the wall, zonk.

**boxed (in)**: to be trapped in a group of riders, unable to move forward or sideways.

**big motor**: 2,200cc motorbike used for outdoor pacing.

**break, breakaway**: one or more cyclists race ahead, splitting the group.

**bridge**: to bridge a gap or cross from one group of cyclists to a group ahead.

**bunch**: the main group of cyclists. *Also* group, field, pack or peloton.

**bunch sprint**: the riders approach the finish line in a large group.

**bunny hop**: to lift both wheels off the ground.

**cadence**: rate of pedalling, measured in revolutions per minute.

**cat, category** (Elite, 1, 2, 3, 4): a ranking system for cyclists in amateur and semi-pro racing, from experienced (Elite) to beginner (Cat 4).

**chain gang**: a group of cyclists who meet for training sessions, usually in pace lines.

**chase**: when a chasing group tries to catch up with a group of riders who have broken away.

**chasers**: those who are trying to catch a group or a lead rider.

**chop**: to move down the track, cutting off another rider (hook is a similar move, but up the track). Penalties include disqualification or suspension.

**chopper**: an erratic, unsafe rider who doesn't hold his line.

**clincher**: conventional tyre with separate inner tube. *Also* wire-on.

**commissaire**: a race judge.

**derny**: a small, pedal-assisted motorcycle used to pace cyclists. Also a name for a motor-paced race.

**drafting**: riding closely behind another cyclist or vehicle to take advantage of the windbreak/slipstream and use less energy. *Also* sitting on a wheel, wheel-sucking.

**dropped**: getting left behind by the group. *Also* out the back.

**drops**: the lower part of down-turned handlebars.

**entraineur**: motor-pace driver.

**false start**: when someone jumps the gun, usually resulting in a restart or disqualification.

**fixed wheel**: a direct-drive set-up using one chain ring and one rear cog; when the rear wheel turns, so does the chain and crank; coasting or freewheeling isn't possible.

**hammer**: to ride hard. *Also* put the hammer down.

**hand-sling**: a grasp of hands as the active rider in a Madison swings his partner into the race.

**hanging in**: barely maintaining contact at the back of the pack.

**hit the wall**: to completely run out of energy. *Also* blow up, bonk, zonk.

**holder**: person who holds the rider at the start of a pursuit or time trial; they do *not* push.

**home straight**: the part of the track where the finish line is situated.

**hook**: to move up the track, cutting off another rider (opposite of a chop). Penalties include disqualification or suspension.

**jam**: a period of hard, fast riding.

**jump**: a quick, hard acceleration without warning, that may develop into a breakaway or sprint, usually standing on the pedals, out of the saddle. *Also* kick.

**kick**: a sudden acceleration, that may be at the beginning or end of a sprint, as in finishing kick.

**leech**: a rider who drafts behind others to reduce his effort, but does not reciprocate. *Also* wheel-sucker.

**lunge**: when a rider thrusts the bike ahead of his body at the finish line, gaining several inches in hopes of winning a close sprint.

**mash**: to push hard on the pedals.

**massed start**: a race start in which riders begin together at the same time and compete head-to-head.

**mechanical**: a problem with the mechanical function of a bicycle, after which a rider may be allowed to restart.

**motor-pace**: to ride behind a motorcycle or other vehicle that acts as a windbreak.

**neutralised**: an inactive period in a race, usually at the start of a bunch endurance race or after a crash, when riders go to the top of the track, ride at a steady pace and maintain their relative position without racing.

**off the back/out the back**: one or more riders who are dropped, or can't keep pace with the main group.

**off the front**: being well ahead of the pack in a race.

**out of the saddle**: standing up on the pedals, off the seat.

**pace line**: a line of riders travelling closely together and taking turns in the lead to save energy.

**pack**: the largest group of riders in a massed-start event. *Also* bunch, group, peloton.

**pacer/pacing**: rider, riders or motorbike acting as a windbreak for a following rider.

**palmares**: a cyclist's list of career wins and honours.

**paniagua**: riding 'clean' or dope-free (Spanish for 'bread and water'). *Also* riding on bread and water.

**peloton**: the whole or main group of cyclists. *Also* bunch, field, pack.

**pick up**: a change of partners in the Madison event.

**prime**: mid-race sprints for prizes, points or time bonuses, to encourage more competitive riding. Primes (pronounced 'preems', after the French word for gift) may be predetermined for certain laps or spontaneously designated by race officials and signalled by a bell on the lap preceding the prime sprint.

**pull**: to take a turn at the front of a group of riders or pace line.

**pull it back**: to work to reduce the lead of a breakaway.

**pull off**: to give up at the front of a group and return to a position further back so another rider can take over. *Also* swing off.

**pull through**: to take the front position in a pace line after the previous leader has pulled off.

**pursuit line**: a white line 20cm from the inner edge of the track, used by pursuit riders.

**pusher**: a person holding, then pushing or shoving the rider at the start of a sprint race.

**red line**: a red line 90cm from the inner edge of the track for sprinters, marking the edge of the sprinter's lane; no following rider should move below the line in the final 200 metres of a race when the lead sprinter is riding on it. *Also* sprinter's line.

**repêchage**: a round in a race series that allows a second chance for losers of early qualifying heats.

**riding on bread and water**: being dope-free. *Also* paniagua.

**rush the gap**: when a chasing rider briefly leaves a gap, then builds sufficient speed to rush past the front rider so he (hopefully) can't get into the slipstream.

**shelled**: to drop out the back of the group. *Also* dropped, left behind.

**sit up**: when a rider eases his efforts and stops pulling or maintaining the pace of the group.

**sit on a wheel**: to ride closely behind the rider immediately in front, in someone's draft. *Also* wheel-sucking.

**slingshot**: to ride up behind another rider with help from his draft, then use the momentum to sprint past.

**smash it**: to go off the front and leave competitors in your wake.

**spin**: pedalling at a rapid cadence.

**spin out**: when a rider has reached the maximum speed for his gearing and can't increase cadence any further.

**sprint lane**: the lane between the inner edge of the track and the red line; while sprinting for the finish the leading rider in this lane 'owns the lane' and can only be passed by a rider going over on the right.

**sprinter's line**: a red line 90cm from the inner edge of the track, marking the edge of the sprinter's lane. *Also* red line.

**stayer**: a motor-pace rider, generally one who competes behind 'big motors'.

**stayer's line**: a blue line one-third of the way up the track from the inside edge marking the boundary between faster and slower traffic, with faster riders below the line and slower riders above the line; in motor-paced events the pacer and his rider (or 'stayer') must keep inside except when overtaking.

**stoker**: the rear cyclist on a tandem.

**swing off**: a cyclist leaving the front of a group after producing his effort by moving up the track. *Also* pull off.

**tandem**: a bicycle built for two or more (traditionally ridden by a 'pilot' or 'captain' at the front and 'stoker' at the back) – the front rider steers while both riders pedal.

**throw the bike**: the rider shoves his arms forward and arches his back, attempting to shunt his bike over the finish line before his competitors.

**tops**: the top part of drop handlebars.

**track stand**: a manoeuvre where the rider stops the bike and attempts to remain standing still, balancing in one spot.

**tubular/tubs**: a lightweight tyre that has its inner tube sewn inside the casing. *Also* sew-up.

**tuck**: a pursuit or time-trial event riding position, with the head and torso low, back flat, and arms close in for aerodynamics.

**wheel-sucker**: a cyclist who sits on the rear wheel of other riders in a pace line or peloton, taking advantage of slipstream but not working. *Also* leech.

**white line**: a white line 20cm from the inner edge, used by pursuit riders: the quickest circuit of the track

**wind up**: accelerate up to top speed.

**zonk**: to suddenly run out of energy and to be unable to continue at the required pace. *Also* blow up, bonk, hit the wall.

# Sources

Bacon, Ellis, *Great British Cycling: The History of British Bike Racing 1868–2014*, Bantam Press (2014)

Boulting, Ned, *On the Road Bike: The Search for a Nation's Cycling Soul*, Yellow Jersey Press (2014)

Dineen, Robert, *Reg Harris: The Rise and Fall of Britain's Greatest Cyclist*, Ebury Press (2012)

Godwin, Tommy, *It Wasn't That Easy: The Tommy Godwin Story*, John Pinkerton Memorial Publishing Fund (2007)

Hampton, Janie, *The Austerity Olympics: When the Games Came to London in 1948*, Aurum Press (2008)

Harris, Reg, *Two Wheels to the Top*, W.H. Allen (1976)

Hayles, Rob, *Easy Rider: My Life on a Bike*, Corgi (2013)

Horton, Dave, Paul Rosen and Peter Cox (eds), *Cycling and Society*, Ashgate (2007)

Mallon, Bill and Ian Buchanan, *The 1908 Olympic Games: Results for All Competitors in All Events, With Commentary*, McFarland (2009)

McGurn, James, *On Your Bicycle*, John Murray (1987)

Moore, Gerry, *The Little Black Bottle: Choppy Warburton,*

*the Question of Doping and the Death of his Bicycle Racers*, Cycle Publishing (2011)

Moore, Richard, *Heroes, Villains and Velodromes: Chris Hoy and Britain's Track Cycling Revolution*, HarperSport (2012)

Nicholson, Geoffrey, *Tony Doyle: Six-Day Rider*, Springfield Books (1992)

Pickering, Edward, *The Race Against Time: Obree, Boardman and the Quest to be the Fastest Man on Two Wheels*, Bantam Press (2013)

Reid, Carlton, *Roads Were Not Built for Cars: How Cyclists Were the First to Push for Good Roads & Became the Pioneers of Motoring*, Island Press (2015)

Sidwells, Chris, *The Long Race to Glory: How the British Came to Rule the Cycling World*, Andre Deutsch (2013)

Simpson, Tommy, *Cycling is My Life*, Yellow Jersey Press (1966)

Thomas, Geraint, *The World of Cycling According to G*, Quercus (2015)

Underwood, Peter, *Dennis Horn: Racing for an English Rose*, Mousehold Press (2013)

Watts, John, *The Good Friday Gamble*, self-published (2003)

Watts, John, *Herne Hill: From Stadium to Velodrome 1891– 2013*, John Pinkerton Memorial Publishing Fund (2013)

Wiggins, Bradley, *In Pursuit of Glory: The Autobiography*, Orion (2008)

Woodland, Les, *This Island Race: Inside 135 Years of British Bike-Racing*, Mousehold Press (2005)

# Index

## About the author

Mark Wellings is a publisher, writer and historian. Born and raised in north-west England, he spent a decade living and working abroad before settling with his family in south-east London – a short ride from Herne Hill Velodrome. A lifelong cyclist, he fell in love with the track the first time he took his young son there and has not looked back: he is now a regular volunteer, spectator and occasional participant. He loves taking his Italian road bikes on iconic rides around Europe, but is usually to be found at the back of the pack on Sunday rides with VC Londres. A risible wheel-sucker, he still dreams of having a double-jump like Reg Harris.